*Just Let Me
Lie Down*

Just Let Me Lie Down

NECESSARY TERMS FOR
THE HALF-INSANE WORKING MOM

Kristin van Ogtrop

Little, Brown and Company
New York Boston London

Little, Brown and Company
Hachette Book Group
237 Park Avenue, New York, NY 10017
www.hachettebookgroup.com

First Edition: April 2010

Little, Brown and Company is a division of Hachette Book Group, Inc. The Little, Brown name and logo are trademarks of Hachette Book Group, Inc.

Library of Congress Cataloging-in-Publication Data
Van Ogtrop, Kristin.
    Just let me lie down : necessary terms for the half-insane working mom / Kristin van Ogtrop. — 1st ed.
        p. cm.
    ISBN 978-0-316-06828-4
    1. Working mothers.   2. Working mothers — Terminology.   I. Title.
    HQ759.48.V34 2010
    306.874'3 — dc22   2009032177

10 9 8 7 6 5 4 3 2 1

RRD-IN

Printed in the United States of America

For Dean and our boys,
who make it possible to love the insanity

"Work and love — these are the basics.
Without them there is neurosis." — THEODOR REIK

Just Let Me Lie Down

A word (or 1,691) about the words in this book

Over the years there have been many ridiculous moments in my life as a working mother, but I suppose the worst was the Hutchinson River Parkway Incident. I was nineteen weeks pregnant with my third child and rushing home from midtown Manhattan to catch the annual Halloween parade at my son's elementary school. I was taking a taxi, something I didn't do very often, but at the time it seemed a wiser choice than the train: I hadn't missed a Halloween parade in seven years and I wasn't about to start.

The driver was a lovely man who, I was later to learn, had four children of his own. He was also, unfortunately, one of those drivers whose foot seems constantly to thump from accelerator to brake and back. You know the type. You probably also know that if you are inclined to throw up, this kind of driving is going to make you throw up faster. But I'm getting ahead of myself.

I felt a bit queasy when I got in the car; I had just eaten an enormous bowl of minestrone before we embarked. As we made our way through Manhattan, acceleratingbraking-acceleratingbraking, the queasiness got worse. I tried focusing on the horizon, closing my eyes, sucking on the cinnamon Tic Tacs I found in the bottom of my purse—nothing worked. I swore to myself that when we got to the Hutchinson River Parkway and ceased with the stop-start driving, everything would be fine.

Alas, everything was not fine. Things went downhill fast when we hit the open road. I croaked, "Sir, I think I'm going to throw up," and the driver screeched across two lanes of traffic and skidded to a stop in the gravel on the side of the road. Just picture an otherwise respectable-looking woman in a pretty silk blazer with a mandarin collar, trying to pretend she was someplace else. Passing motorists no doubt glanced over and said to themselves, "Oh, go home and sleep it off, you old drunk." Except for passing motorists who happened to be women; those drivers looked over and said to themselves, "Oh, poor thing. She's just a half-insane pregnant working mom, trying to make it to the Halloween parade."

And that, dear reader, is the work-life balance at its best.

Maybe the most annoying part is that it was the *only* time I threw up during that pregnancy. The only time! At nineteen weeks! Naturally, I blame it on Halloween itself (see *Take Halloween, for example,* p. 205). The driver was kind and understanding and went on to tell me about his wife and her four pregnancies filled with morning sickness and that the only person who had ever thrown up in his car was Paris Hilton's boyfriend. Which for some reason—even though I can't for the life of me remember my checking account number—I have not forgotten to this day. I made the parade, and I was only five minutes late. A small triumph in the life of this half-insane working mom.

Five lessons to be learned from the Hutchinson River Parkway Incident:

- You can throw up in the second trimester, even if you didn't in the first.
- Tic Tacs are pretty much worthless: too small to be a legitimate breath mint, and they don't prevent vomiting.
- Halloween is just a nightmare on so many levels.
- There is often an empathetic older gentleman nearby when you are in distress.
- Things work out in the end, if you have the right perspective.

That last lesson is the key, of course, for anybody trying to fit a demanding job and a demanding family into the same life. But how did I get to that place: a respectable woman, throwing up on the side of the road in my silk jacket with the mandarin collar?

My story is like that of so many women I know, and it goes something like this: You were an overachiever from the time you were in diapers, always trying your hardest, nose to the grindstone, if at first you didn't succeed...you know how it goes. Maybe you got a little wild in your early twenties, but really, just a little—it's not like you ever got arrested for anything. Then you calmed down and got married and landed a great job and eventually had kids and everything was going along just fine until *BAM* came the day when you didn't quite know how to communicate a very basic thing to your child's babysitter. You could hire people and fire people and control budgets and manage up and manage down in the working world, but you couldn't figure out an effective, kind, nonjudgmental way to tell your babysitter that it's actually not a great idea to let your toddler go to nursery school when he has pinkeye. Suddenly you wonder: What is wrong with you? Why didn't they offer a college course in *that*?

Like any good student, all my life I have relied on reference books, guidebooks, dictionaries, illustrated histories, you name it. My whole existence can be charted by books like *Our Bodies, Ourselves; Your Pregnancy Week by Week; What to Expect the Toddler Years; Labrador Retrievers for Dummies;* even that collection of *New York Times* real-estate-section columns detailing all the places to live in the Greater New York City area (which, in retrospect, doesn't really tell you any of the important things, like whether your neighbors will plant lots of ugly, brightly colored plastic toys in the front yard). Whatever life threw at me, I've always navigated it with a handy book.

But when you are throwing up by the side of the Hutchinson River Parkway, or trying to write a note to a babysitter who doesn't realize you can practically transmit pinkeye by looking at somebody the wrong way... well, there's just no guidebook for that. There appears to be a mystifying and completely unhelpful hole in the reference-book canon when it comes to mostly happy but partly crazy working moms and their daily lives.

I was in a meeting the other day when a colleague remarked that for women, the whole working-versus-not-working tension was "over." Women today just "do their thing," he said, and the assignment for all of us, whether we are working or not, is to find our own happiness in a landscape that is wide open. Like millions of women, I think I've found that happiness, even if it means I have given up half my sanity in exchange. I am extremely lucky, blessed with a job I love and a family I love even more. I complain that my job gets in the way of so many things I want to do, but it also helps me forget the chaos that reigns in my very old house, filled as it is with three rambunctious boys (ages fourteen, eleven, and two—not a typo; see *Accounting error,* p. 14), a fairly messy husband, a giant shedding dog and an elderly cat, hamsters and fish that quickly come and go, and various unwanted representatives of the wild kingdom (including a renegade squirrel that once actually ran down the stairs of the house and into the room where I was standing, an episode that is too painful and embarrassing to include in this book).

Particulars of my life aside, there are countless mothers just like me. Women who want to succeed at work and do what's best for their children, and who—when those two goals seem to be most at odds—find a way to flip the disadvantage. Women who know perfection is a concept but never a goal, who know there are as many ways to be a good mother as there are to get promoted or avoid going to the gym. And there is a lingua franca that connects us, helping us through the times when the school secretary calls at the office because we forgot to give our kid lunch money, or the babysitter calls because she can't find the light saber that goes with the Luke Skywalker costume, or we're trying to answer work e-mails by BlackBerry (which certain children, not mentioning any names, call "the family killer") as we speed to a weekend soccer game. There are things we do because we love our families and there are things we do because we love our jobs, and sometimes these things try to cancel each other out.

Motherhood and working are journeys of trial and error, and even after years of experimentation and analysis and data points, you sometimes feel like you know less than you did when you started. I for one know less about the following: why boys always say "Nothing" when you ask what they did at school that day; why husbands never turn off the TV; why you can't fire someone just for being irritating. But I do know a few things, starting with the fact that a good many working mothers could use some sort of organizing principle, a few labeled bins to hold the chaos. Hence this collection: an alphabetically arranged dictionary of terms, observations, lists, complaints, questions, musings, and the occasional diatribe about the little joys and major nonsense that define life for me, and untold women like me, on a daily basis.

Now for the caveat: although my path through adulthood has been fairly traditional, I do not presume to speak for all working mothers. In my life, hard work (and luck) have reaped real rewards, and not everyone is so fortunate. My husband is remarkably tolerant, and when my children are annoying, it rarely lasts long. Because my struggles are not all that serious, and almost entirely self-induced, I try to laugh when things go wrong (unless I am too tired to laugh, which leads to charmless and unattractive outbursts that I usually regret later). I hope this book allows you to recognize your own daily struggles and to respond to them with a laugh. And if you are too tired to laugh, well, I recommend lying down and trying to squeeze in a little nap, before everyone around you starts to protest.

Absentee parenthood
Accounting error
Actually
Adding insult to injury
"Area of opportunity"
Automatic writing

Absentee parenthood: The state of being that sometimes defines your life and is by turns depressing and wonderful.

There are wonderful things about being an absentee parent, namely taking business trips that involve staying in a hotel room all by yourself, or having vital work meetings that keep you from going on the field trip to the local recycling plant, or being generally much too busy to bake anything for Teacher Appreciation Week. Yes, it's possible that other mothers will whisper about what a slacker you are, but you just need to learn to live with that.

But there are depressing moments too, and they can come when you least expect them. Once I was walking to school with my middle son, something we do nearly every day despite the fact that he would much prefer to be driven. I was leaving for a long business trip the following morning, and as my son launched into his routine anti-walking complaint (note: school is all of six blocks away), I said brightly, "Just think! Tomorrow I will be in California, and Daddy will drive you to school for the rest of the week!" My son looked crestfallen. "Oh no," he said. "That means I'll have to eat breakfast in the car, and I *hate* eating breakfast in the car." And as much as I was looking forward to sleeping in a giant hotel bed all by myself, not to mention taking two long flights with no phone or e-mail access, the breakfast-in-the-car comment did dampen my enthusiasm. It may have been my son's way of telling me without telling me that he was going to miss his mother, or perhaps he just didn't want to have to eat breakfast in under seven minutes and arrive at school with peanut butter on his face. Depending on my state of mind (see *Guilt curve,* p. 83), I could interpret it either way.

Accounting error: The irrevocable mistake you make when you decide to have one more child than you can actually handle, which pushes the parental sanity balance sheet from the black (a place of comfort, if occasional boredom) to the red (excitement, panic).

A few years ago I happened upon the book *Where There's a Will* by John Mortimer. In one particularly delightful passage he explained the necessity of always having a child around the house. I realized I couldn't have agreed more, which led to the ruination of the family balance sheet, in the form of a midlife-crisis baby.

Our midlife-crisis baby arrived three weeks before my forty-third birthday, when I was still forty-two, which seems more than a year younger than forty-three when you're dealing with matters of reproduction. My husband and I had talked for the better part of a decade about whether or not to have a third child; the first child and even the second were no-brainers, but deciding to have a third was really a *commitment*. No doubt some of my reluctance came from my mother's cautionary words: "Having two is like having one and a half, but having three is like having ten." (And this from a woman who could actually take care of three young daughters, throw dinner parties, and sew clothes, all in the same day.) I had had two miscarriages when I was thirty-nine, which left me wary. After producing my first two children with tremendous luck and efficiency, the back-to-back miscarriages were a giant surprise that resulted in a lot of sadness on the part of me and my husband and a lot of tears on the part of me. I felt jinxed, and I was not eager to repeat the experience.

As time passed, I began to view the miscarriages as the inevitable result of (1) a lack of enthusiasm on my part, and (2) God's conviction that the whole third-child thing was a really bad idea for me. But the sense that someone was missing just wouldn't go away. One day I explained the God theory to my husband, who replied, "Well, maybe God was testing you, to see how much you wanted it." This confused me a great deal. What if he was right? When I turned forty-two I made a decision: I did not want to turn fifty-two and still be wondering if we should have another child. Having a third was also appealing in terms of my midlife-crisis options. Compared to Botox, plastic surgery, a convertible, or an affair, a baby seemed like an eminently healthy choice — no sneaking around, no facial injections, no having to run out and put the top up if it started to rain.

So that was it. I informed God of my decision but didn't let my husband know for a couple of months. I told him on our fifteenth anniversary, and I think I was pregnant about four minutes later. This time, miraculously, everything stuck: I did not have a miscarriage and the baby was not born with two heads. Given my "advanced maternal age" (honestly, can't someone think of a better term?), each new test that came back normal was an unbelievable gift, like getting a horse for Christmas when you're twelve. The day my third son was born felt like the luckiest day of my whole life.

One very nice thing about having a baby once your career is pretty much established is that you don't worry nearly as much about how your pregnancy will affect your ascension to whatever height you're aiming for. People around you marvel at how relaxed you are about the whole thing; they chalk it up to the wisdom of experience, and you don't have the heart to tell them that you're simply exhausted and just don't give a damn unless something is on fire. And when you have an established, demanding career, maternity leave actually feels like a vacation. Which is perverse.

So now I have three children, with an eight-year gap between the last two and ovaries that got the job done in the nick of time. Regarding having one child too many, and a life that is perhaps 25 percent too chaotic, friends told me, "Once he's here, you won't be able to remember what things were like without him." That is not entirely true. I clearly remember being able to sit down with a glass of wine before dinner on Sunday night and read a book. I also remember sleeping past 7:30, having stairways in my house that were not blocked by ugly baby gates, and being able to decorate our Christmas tree with an overall symmetry in mind, rather than with the need to keep all breakable ornaments clustered at the top. You are not supposed to admit this sort of thing when you have a baby in your forties, because if you are able to bear a child at an age when half of your contemporaries are either having hot flashes or getting fertility treatments, you should just be grateful and shut up about it. But no matter how old or grateful you are, there really are benefits to not having a toddler around.

Now, other friends told me, "Once he's here, you won't doubt your decision for an instant." And, whether or not our balance sheet has gone permanently into the red, that part is absolutely right.

Actually: One of the top five most dangerous words in the English language. Beware any sentence that begins with "actually," as in "Actually, we've decided to eliminate your whole department" or "Actually, I don't think it's the best haircut you've ever had." Other dangerous sentence starters: "I've done a lot of thinking" and "Mom, don't be mad."

Adding insult to injury: When, after you've gone jogging for the first time in years and can barely make it up the stairs the next day, your husband — who may genuinely think he's being helpful — observes: "You really should find time to work out more."

"Area of opportunity": The silly euphemism a boss or human resources representative uses when there's something about your performance that needs improving. After all, an "area of opportunity" sounds a lot more palatable than "the thing you seem incapable of doing." However, I would suggest that *areas of opportunity* not be limited to the workplace. I have several *areas of opportunity* for the children I live with:

- Feeding the cat before he starts meowing like he has his tail caught in a door—a meow that only your mother seems to hear
- Reading a book instead of playing on the computer every chance you get
- Putting your shoes in the closet, rather than right in the middle of the doorway, where you are inconveniencing even yourself
- Stepping outside to feel the temperature before declaring that you don't need a coat
- Cleaning out your fish tank before your whole bedroom begins to smell
- Showering, for once in your life, without your mother having to insist

Automatic writing: A trancelike state in which you have no control over what you are communicating. William Butler Yeats's wife thought she could pull this off and so can you, only in your life "automatic writing" means dashing off an e-mail on your BlackBerry while leaning on the kitchen counter, with someone standing next to you begging for a peanut butter sandwich. And so the e-mail makes very little sense, if you're even sending it to the right person. (Just ask my sister about the time she sent confidential company information to her neighbor Michael Bacon instead of to her coworker Michael Salmon.)

Balancing act
Benign neglect
Best of luck
Book of Too Much
Border collie disease
Boredom fantasy
Borrowed time
Brain spins

Balancing act: A hilarious notion that some feminist (or come to think of it, it may have been an antifeminist) came up with to describe what any working mother must do: that is, bring home the bacon and fry it up in a pan. But the skillet is very, very heavy, and on certain days you don't even feel like you can pick it up. Other days you'd like to use it as a weapon — and would, if it didn't mean certain arrest, which would have negative playground ramifications for your kids. On these days you really are just acting, to very little applause.

Benign neglect: The Bad Mother habits you eventually allow yourself to fall into once you've gotten all of the hypervigilant, 100 percent organic goody-two-shoes-ism out of the way with your first child.

Because I had our last son when I was forty-two, most kids his age have mothers who are younger than I am. The downside to this is that people might eventually come to mistake me for his grandmother. The upside is that I think I understand some things better than my younger counterparts. An example: a couple of weeks ago I was at the nursery school fair with our two-year-old and he wanted a snack. Naturally I bought him a chocolate-covered chocolate doughnut. Yes, there were healthier choices, although not many, because other parents had very sensibly already chosen those healthy things. But the chocolate-covered chocolate doughnut was what my son pointed at. I imagined the stares of judgment and horror on the faces of my (less-experienced) fellow moms, and I wanted to put a sign on my back: "I am also the mother of a fourteen-year-old. Trust me: a chocolate doughnut does not really matter."

Best of luck: The happy realization that you have accidentally stumbled upon a career that you really love.

A couple of years ago my friend Cindi had lunch with a phenomenally successful businessman who runs an international company that his family built from scratch. He told her at lunch that what she needed—what, in fact, everyone needs—is a five-year plan with clear, attainable goals. Cindi, who is a fellow magazine editor, recounted this advice to me and I immediately went into a tailspin. I've never had a five-year plan! I've never had goals! For example, right now all I know is that within five years I would really, really like to renovate our master bathroom and find a way to get the washer and dryer upstairs so I don't ever again have to go down into our creepy basement, which is something straight out of *The Silence of the Lambs*. I'd also like to figure out how I can make my children hang their coats on the designated hooks by the back door instead of just throwing them on the floor every time they enter the house, and I could seriously use a better face cream with SPF. As for five-year goals, that's about it.

Goals were just never on the menu for me (see *"Not on the menu,"* p. 147), perhaps because my entire career was an accident from the start. I grew up in a household where my mom stayed at home with the kids until I was in high school and my father said things like "Why do you think they call it 'work'?" My dad complained frequently about his job, even though he was (and still is) diligent about doing it well. Still, I can't count the number of times he told me and my two sisters, "Girls, whatever you do, don't become lawyers." But what was I to become instead? In high school I was a good student, sure, but what I mostly liked to do in my spare time was write letters to my friend Anne Bardsley, pretending to be a character from a book we'd had to read for English class (my personal favorite was Mrs. Manson Mingott from *The Age of Innocence*), or stare moonily out my bedroom window, listening to Janis Ian records and wondering if I'd ever find true love. What kind of career did that set me up for?

After a brief flirtation with premed that ended in Cs in every math and science class I took, I majored in English. Because they are good parents, my mom and dad were supportive, but underneath their enthusiasm and encouragement, the fact that I was an English major (impractical!) nearly killed them. Maybe I would read a lot of good books, but I'd certainly never have two dimes to rub together. As I continued through college and then graduate school (for a master's degree in English—unspeakably impractical!), I was surrounded by lawyers: my father, my boyfriend's father, my two best friends. After graduate school, as I jumped from one bad impulse of a job to another, I did think, *Oh hell, maybe I should just go to law school.* But I knew I would hate it: I am not patient, I am not analytical, I'm probably not smart enough, and I really don't like to read anything that doesn't have the occasional exclamation point. In fact the only thing about being a lawyer that I'd be good at would be writing on those wonderful, long yellow legal pads that my father brought home with him by the dozen. (They certainly worked for Mrs. Manson Mingott.)

Then a friend of a (lawyer) friend got me an interview at Condé Nast Publications, and the next thing I knew I had an entry-level job at *Vogue*. Never mind that I had never really followed fashion and could not name any of the reigning supermodels. Within my first couple of months, one of the editors wore a bikini top to work. A bikini top! That's when I knew things were going to be interesting. Now, the more practical among us might argue that people who wear bikini tops to work are frivolous and possibly insane; I would argue that people who wear bikini tops to work are *fascinating.* And is there anything better than being surrounded by fascinating people?

Fast-forward through four magazines and nineteen years, and here I am. Although I didn't set out to have a magazine career, per se, if you keep doing something because you like it and suddenly a decade or two passes—well, you have a career. In my line of work I am surrounded by people who are funny and creative and collaborative and have very few temper tantrums or fits of ego. There are highly successful women everywhere I look, and nobody makes enough money to think she is all-powerful or exempt from the common rules of human decency, the plague of Wall Street and Hollywood. I do work for a large corporation, which means that there is a degree of bureaucratic b.s. that must be endured or, if you have the right attitude, actually enjoyed (see *Corporate takeover,* p. 42). But it is rare that I find myself in a work situation that is boring; my work life feels like a giant jigsaw puzzle of something gorgeous and delicious, like a huge chocolate cupcake. Sometimes I will be in a meeting, having a very serious discussion about something like, well, cupcakes, or Facebook, or stain removal, or fake plants, all in the name of work, and I will think to myself, *Thank God I never really had to become an adult.*

My friend Elizabeth, a successful corporate lawyer and mother of four, once said, in describing my job, "Kristin talks about colors all day." I just smiled, because she's right. Isn't that amazing? I still can't believe I get paid for it.

Book of Too Much: The overkill that occurs when you think more of a good thing is always better. I learned this concept from a stylish saleswoman who once helped me find some maternity clothes that I could bear to wear to work. I tried on a particular outfit that I thought was sort of cute. "Oh no," she said, clucking her tongue. "Now you are going to the Book of Too Much." This concept also comes in handy when describing boneheaded ideas or micromanaging colleagues or children who think it's perfectly fine to drink Gatorade followed by Capri Sun followed by Vitamin Water followed by Sprite, with no milk anywhere in sight.

Border collie disease: An affliction that affects some of your coworkers, although you are the one who suffers. Symptoms include excessive barking, nipping at your heels, attempts to herd you in a particular direction even though you know exactly where you're headed. Your only defense: bleat angrily and run away as fast as you can.

Boredom fantasy: When you think longingly back to the time when you were fifteen and had nothing to do but lie around the house obsessing over the fact that you would never have long, beautiful fingernails, hair like Claire Fleming's, or a boyfriend. You were just bored bored bored, waiting for your real life to start. Now that you are older and have a husband and kids and can even pay for a manicure, you would give almost anything to have enough free time to be bored. Just for one afternoon.

Borrowed time: The sad reality that, more often than not, it is the people around you who are really in charge of your schedule. Therefore, if you want any time for yourself—to go to the gym, say, or spend your lunch hour at your desk shopping online—you need to "borrow" the time from someone who thinks they have a more important claim to it. This sad reality has led to countless magazine articles in which experts advise you to "schedule me-time" or "put fun on your calendar," which, if nothing else, at least give you a chuckle.

Brain spins: The unpleasant phenomenon that occurs when you wake up at 3:15 a.m. and start thinking about the work meeting you are dreading tomorrow, whether or not your son will remember that he needs to take an empty two-liter soda bottle to school for a science experiment—wait, do we even *have* any two-liter soda bottles?!—and if you should nag your husband again about your family's lack of a summer vacation plan or just take the whole project over yourself. No matter what your to-do list looks like, you will not fall back to sleep until 4:45, and then you'll be woken up by your alarm at 6:00.

Caller ID malfunction
Child abuse (harmless)
Child abuse (harmful)
Child-care provider
Close encounters of the half-insane kind
Clothes make the woman
        ...want to blow up the whole house
Cognitive dissonance
Comfort station
Cone of silence
Confidence man
Conflict of interest
Corporate seepage
Corporate takeover
Coup de moi
Creative control
Critical mass

Caller ID malfunction: When you have dialed a number and cannot remember whom it belongs to, but the phone is ringing and it feels too late to hang up, in case someone has gotten up out of a chair on the other end to answer your call. Are you calling the pediatrician? Your boss? The plumber? It's anybody's guess.

Child abuse (harmless): When you are talking to a childless person who's irritating you, and you start telling stories about your children to get rid of him. This does not always work, but when it does it's a marvel.

Child abuse (harmful): When you are talking to any sort of person, childless or otherwise, and you launch into a long/boring/pointless story about your children that is of no interest to anyone but you and perhaps one or two members of your immediate family. If the person has good manners, he will nod and smile, but beware: his opinion of you is rapidly plummeting.

Child-care provider: A term usually meant as a politically correct catchall for any kind of babysitter (day-care center employee, nanny, au pair). To this limited list I would add:

- Anyone who entertains your child at a restaurant, whether it's someone blowing up balloons in the shape of animals or just a friendly occupant of the booth behind you who genuinely does not mind your toddler peering over her shoulder.
- The stranger in the mall who tells you that your baby's pacifier has fallen out of the stroller.
- The sympathetic fellow mom at the pool who sees that you forgot sunscreen and offers to share hers.
- Anyone who lends a hand when you are flying alone with an infant, like the kindly older man who helped my sister by holding her two-month-old all the way from San Francisco to New York, which is all the proof you need that the world is not a horrible place.

Close encounters of the half-insane kind: Those times when a working mother is seen out of context and mistaken for some other sort of extraterrestrial or unidentified species by the humans who encounter her.

One example: My friend Kris was lying on the grass outside her new house on a warm Saturday when, without intending to, she fell asleep. She has two young daughters and works like a maniac and, like so many overextended moms, can fall asleep anytime she finds herself in a horizontal position (see

Very, verrryyyyy sleeeeeeepy..., p. 224). Kris was wearing a poncho, which she had pulled up over her face, unintentionally creating a headless effect. She doesn't know how long she was asleep, but eventually she began to feel something hitting her body: pebbles, thrown by a group of boys she didn't know, all hovering at a safe distance. As they stared at each other, the groggy busy mom and the pack of boys, one boy called out, "Are you an alien?"

Another example: my sister Valerie threw a *Star Wars* birthday party for her youngest son when he turned five. She held the party in her driveway, complete with the *Star Wars* soundtrack playing on outside speakers. She had somehow found life-sized cardboard cutouts of C-3PO and R2-D2, and every kid got a Darth Vader mask and a light saber.

Valerie is a lot of fun, very creative, and up to any challenge (particularly when working-mother guilt leads her to overcompensate), so naturally she dressed as Princess Leia for the occasion, in a cream bathrobe with a big suede belt, large gold hoop earrings, and brown Birkenstock sandals. She braided her hair and coiled it on both sides of her head, and she carried a light saber tucked into the belt. Valerie is blond, but other than her hair color I have no doubt that she was the spitting image of Princess L. herself.

My sister works full-time and does not know all the parents of her sons' friends. In particular, she has not met many of the fathers. When one dad, whose name is John, dropped off his son in Valerie's driveway, he looked at her strangely. Val found him nice but rather...remote. Later she learned why:

after drop-off, John called his wife with concern. "I think the mom forgot about the party," he told her. "She was still in her pajamas."

Clothes make the woman...want to blow up the whole house: The irritating reality that unless you have a live-in laundress/ seamstress/personal organizer, you will never, ever feel "in control" of your children's clothes, in part because they variously reproduce, migrate, and transmogrify every night when you are asleep.

My children's clothing is such a nightmare, I hardly know where to begin. Our house is overflowing with boys' clothes of every shape and size, and yet our kids basically wear the same three things every single day. One child pays no attention to what he has on and just grabs the item closest to the top of the drawer, which means that more often than not he's wearing pants that have giant holes in the knees and are an inch too short, paired with a just-out-of-season shirt in a clashing shade. Another child hates everything he owns except certain items that have passed some sort of test, which seems to involve a complicated formula of color multiplied by size multiplied by number of times the item has been worn in the privacy of our house. Very, very few articles of clothing pass the test, and so very few items can be worn in public. And then there's our youngest, who does not yet notice what he's wearing, which is a good thing because it means he does not realize (1) how many of his clothes (and stains) have been handed down from two brothers and three cousins, and (2) how often his brothers dress him in their favorite shirt, the black one with "LAVA MAN! HE'S RED HOT!!!" on the front.

The net result is that all of my boys project the same message: *our mother does not care how we look*. Which, sad to say, is pretty close to the truth. When you take a mom (me) who was raised on regular doses of "pretty is as pretty does" by her own mother, and add a demanding work-life tightrope walk, clothes just do not make the list of Life's Most Important Things. Plus, I'm too lazy to keep up with the constant, tedious moving of clothes in and out of dresser drawers that children who won't stop growing seems to involve. Maybe *What to Expect When You're Expecting* should focus a lot less on unimportant things like how your body changes during pregnancy and whether or not you'll survive childbirth, and a lot more on the really painful issues, like the fact that your kids' clothes are always too small/too big/too stained/nowhere to be found, and that every boy between the ages of five and fifteen thinks that putting dirty clothes *next to* the hamper is the same thing as putting clothes inside it.

What's that? Quit complaining about it and get my act together? Oh, I try, but I am not woman enough to conquer the clothing problem. Just this morning our middle son needed black pants and a white dress shirt for the fifth-grade play, and the thought of having to find two specific items that do indeed exist in our household but are not part of the regular clothing rotation almost made me ask my husband for a divorce. And we're not even going to talk about how our son's hair looked when he left the house (on the day of the play, no less). Apparently I don't care enough about grooming either.

Cognitive dissonance: When you insist that you have no ambivalence about being a working mother but your actions or appearance indicates otherwise.

A few years back there was a period when my sister Claire moved around quite a bit as her husband finished graduate school and entered the workforce. During this time she had two babies and continued her psychotherapy career, which is no picnic when you move from state to state, because you have to keep getting relicensed, or some other awful thing that I have blocked out and hope never happens to me. Anyway, when they finally settled down long enough to buy a house, Claire networked for a few months and found a group practice that she wanted to join. Claire is nothing if not a good student, and she had done sufficient homework to know that this was exactly the group for her. Before the interview, Claire's daughter gave her a bead necklace that said "Mom" on it for good luck, which Claire dutifully put on before she left the house. She took the necklace off in the car, as any woman in her right mind would. Somehow, though, the necklace attached itself to a button on the back of Claire's pants, which one of the interviewers pointed out. Oh, the horror. And I forgot to mention that she had pinkeye that day too.

The best part of the whole story? They loved her.

Comfort station: The dead-endish job you stay in longer than you should because it allows you important lifestyle benefits, such as the ability to leave at 5:15 every day or to "work from home" whenever you have a parent-teacher conference in the middle of the day, even though you could go in to the office if you just made the slightest effort.

Cone of silence: The device used by the very best teachers to keep to themselves all your unflattering family secrets, which, if revealed, would prove to your entire school community that you are not the wonderful parent you're cracked up to be, even if you do get your kids to school on time at least three days out of five.

Case in point: My friend Chrissie is a mother of four who returned to work when her youngest child was in preschool. Every day for a week, her daughter would come home from school with a picture she had drawn, complete with a caption she had dictated to the preschool teacher. Sometimes it was a drawing of a store, sometimes of a child sitting at a kitchen table. Every day the teacher wrote the same caption: "Mommy, please go to the grocery store!"

Now, the fact that Chrissie seemed to have no food in the house had nothing to do with financial difficulties, or lack of love for her family. It was just that she had no time for the grocery store in her new working life.

This embarrassing episode could have played out a couple of ways, one of which might have involved some sort of child protective agency. But because the teacher respected the cone of silence, Chrissie never heard a word about it from the school. Or (always the most horrifying prospect) from the parents of the other children. But her three older kids gave her hell about it for weeks.

I'd like to take this opportunity to extend my heartfelt thanks to all those teachers who kept their judgments to themselves when one of my children didn't have lunch money or snow boots, showed up at school with dog hair all over his clothes, or announced, at the age of ten, that *Arrested Development* was his favorite TV show.

Confidence man: The guy in your life—it may be your husband, it may be your father, it may be your best friend—who believes in you above all others, thinks you are smart and beautiful, and loves you despite your manifold flaws. I will not go to the "wind beneath my wings" place here, but I'm tempted, because inside every successful, accomplished, superstar working mother there is a woman who wonders the following:

- How do I ever know if I've made the right choices?
- Are my kids going to hate me in twenty years? In five?
- Do most of my coworkers think I'm an idiot?
- Can love handles *ever* be attractive on a woman?

Maybe the working mother wonders these things once every six months, maybe once every six hours. For the most part, if she is self-actualized enough, she can dismiss her insecurities without assistance. But it is nice to get a little help, especially from the guy who also has seen firsthand, over and over again, all of the things that are wrong with you, and will helpfully point them out if asked.

A little story about my husband. A few months ago I had to do a 360 evaluation at work, which is basically just a chance for your colleagues to let you know — anonymously — how wonderful you are, or how deeply flawed you are, or both. When I got the written report I immediately took it home, in the hopes of showing everybody in my house that I'm not the nincompoop they often mistake me for. I loudly announced that the 360 evaluation had arrived, and my children dove for it, flipped immediately to the part that detailed the ways in which I need to improve (see *"Area of opportunity,"* p. 18), laughed uproariously, quoted a few particularly negative passages, and then went back to whatever it was they were doing. The evaluation then sat on the kitchen counter for a couple of hours, during which time my husband walked by it, oh, twenty-five times without so much as a second glance. It was killing me! I was the eight-year-old girl who had brought home a great report card and Dad couldn't care less. Finally, abandoning all sense of maturity and pride, I asked, "Don't you want to look at my three sixty? People actually had really nice things to say." To which he replied, "I'd be surprised if they didn't." And that is exactly why he is my confidence man: he does not have to read my 360. He already knows what it says, even before I do.

Conflict of interest: It's Sunday: You must take the dog to the park before 9:00 a.m., when he is allowed to be off the leash. Husband has soccer from 9:00 to 10:00; teenager has church confirmation class, also from 9:00 to 10:00. Teenager must be at soccer game one town over at 10:30. Middle child has church school from 10:00 to 11:00. Middle has to be at soccer at 2:30 for a 3:00 game; you have to meet two other members of the fifth-grade yearbook committee, which you volunteered for in a moment of delusion or drunkenness. Husband has Ultimate Frisbee at 3:30, but you're not even discussing that. The two older boys have tennis from 5:00 to 7:00 p.m. Someplace in there the youngest has to take a nap. And is anybody making dinner?

Corporate seepage: The disturbing habit you sometimes fall into when the words you use at work spill over into your personal life. The other night I said to my husband, "I'm going to power through dinner so I can get to that meeting." He said that if I uttered the phrase "power through" one more time, he was going to "close the loop" on our marriage. If you use any of the following words or phrases at home, you are experiencing corporate seepage: "out of pocket," "offline," "synergy," "granular," "incentivize," "interface."

Corporate takeover: The seismic change that occurs when the quasi hippie you once were turns into a functional cog in a giant industrial machine.

A few weeks ago I was on the phone with a working mom

I know, Lani, an energetic, tough New Yorker who spends her days as a partner in a giant law firm, alternately poring over complicated contracts and negotiating with people on behalf of her clients. As we were talking, I heard tinny music erupt from her cell phone in the background. The song was vaguely familiar. "What is your ringtone?" I asked. "The Grateful Dead," she replied.

Ah, I thought, *a kindred spirit.* I did not question her further about the ringtone or find out exactly when it was that she retired the tie-dye and crossed over, for two reasons: one, she bills by the hour, and two, I feel like I could probably write her story myself.

I work in a building that has forty-six floors, on a block full of enormous buildings. With the exception of the architecturally interesting fountains dotting the blocks around me, there is very little evidence of nonrectangular life in my immediate workday surroundings. Sometimes when I am walking into my office I imagine what I look like from a bird's-eye view: a little hurrying speck surrounded by other hurrying specks, moving en masse into a huge, glossy box to make widgets all day.

I didn't used to be a speck hurrying into a glossy box. I was my own person! A free spirit! I wasn't afraid of anyone or anything and thought I had just the right gimlet-eyed approach to life. I couldn't imagine working for a big corporation because it would mean kowtowing to idiots who wore high-waisted pants and possessed no imagination. I was going to...well, I wasn't really sure what I was going to do. But I could tell you one thing: I was never going to be a corporate drone.

Now I work for a company that has three thousand employees. I have goals — with "metrics," which as far as I'm concerned is not a real word — that lead to performance reviews that directly affect the amount of money I make every year. A former English major who can still recite the beginning of *The Canterbury Tales* from memory, I now actually spend part of my waking hours thinking about shareholders and stock prices. I am a small part of a big enterprise that was built to be more than the sum of its parts, a fact I can usually appreciate without rolling my eyes.

So what happened? Where did that other girl go, the one with the "Save the Whales" bumper sticker on her car, who made serious, defining pronouncements like "I will never color my hair!" and meant it, at least at the time? Well, she went to college and got a D+ in economics, which was the first little warning bell that not caring a whit about money might have consequences. Then she had a wedding that produced surprisingly fancy presents, which seemed to require a fairly nice apartment and a grown-up-looking life to support them. She had a child, and learned just how much those boring, necessary things like diapers cost. Along the way she found a career that she loved that happened to involve working for one big company after another (see *Best of luck,* p. 24). But finally, and most important, she realized that in many areas of life you have to work within the system, and that you can do it without your soul turning completely black.

My younger self would be so disappointed in the middle-aged me. Per the strict, callow standards of my younger self, my adult life can be described in one word: *Faustian*. But what my younger self didn't realize was that there are tangible benefits to making a deal with a corporate devil, and that you can define yourself within the system, instead of letting the system define you. Obviously, it's all about perspective. I do not think I'm saving the world when I produce my particular widget. But I am providing useful information and connecting with women across the country, and on the best days that does feel mildly noble. There is something fascinating about making a product that you are trying to get the masses to fall in love with, whether it's a magazine or toothpaste or canned soup. And working toward a common goal with all types of people is endlessly interesting, because whether you know anything about psychology or not, on some level every day is a field trip into the loony bin. There is, as they say, never a dull moment.

So note to my younger self: I do still like the Grateful Dead, although my current ringtone comes from Guns N' Roses, as a tribute to my Axl Rose–loving children. And I do color my hair, like 90 percent of the women I know. If that means we're all shallow—well, I'd rather be shallow than have mousy hair.

Coup de moi: A concept my friend Raylene cooked up with a massage therapist, when she was in the middle of her own coup de moi. It works like this: There is a flag football game at 6:30 at night and the entire family is going, but it's November and thirty-five degrees outside and you declare in a moment of bravery at 6:15, *I am not going. My son will just have to know that I love him.* No one protests and you end up on the sofa with a glass of wine in a completely quiet house. That is a coup de moi. Or you look at your work schedule for the day and see that it contains three meetings that don't need to happen and so you cancel them. That is a coup de moi. Or you keep getting cc'd on a long, tedious e-mail chain and finally send out a reply-to-all that says, "Please stop cc'ing me or I'm going to kill one of you"—coup de moi!

Creative control: A state of being that is crucial to the sanity of any functional working mother: knowing when to micromanage, when to let go, and tricky ways to *appear* to let go while continuing to micromanage.

Face it: You cannot, realistically, be at every single elementary school function. You cannot, realistically, be on every board or committee that affects your children. And you cannot drop everything to go to Old Navy on a Tuesday afternoon when it is communicated to you in no uncertain terms that your teenager does not have a single pair of jeans that are long enough, and he hates all the clothes in his drawers.

Like most mothers, I have a bizarre and random list of mundane things that signal a loss of control in my life:

- My kids' fingernails are too long.
- There are dirty diapers piled on top of the Diaper Genie because they no longer fit inside.

- We have forgotten to take the recycling to the curb for three straight weeks.
- There is no more milk in the refrigerator.
- Four half-empty Gatorade bottles are rolling around on the floor of the car.

I try to overlook these things and focus on the bigger picture—the ongoing decision-making about whether something matters enough for me to attempt to control it. Every working mother has her own list of things she is willing to delegate or let go of completely without feeling that she has relinquished her spot at the top of the household. It has taken me years to get to this place, but I have finally figured out which things I can delegate and which I can just let go of completely.

Delegate:
- Taking my children to get their hair cut (unless it is baby's first appointment or a cut of equal significance)
- Taking the pets to the vet
- All trips to Costco

Give up on completely:
- Making birthday cakes from scratch
- Writing a personal message on every Christmas card
- Cleaning my own windows
- Making my own bread, even though I do own a bread machine

Now, this is not to say that I do not prefer to take my kids for haircuts, or that I don't appreciate homemade bread. It's just that I have learned to give up those things without feeling like I am an absolute failure as a parent, a woman, and a human being.

Critical mass: When, after years of sitting at a desk every day, your rear end finally gets big enough that you must face the truth: it's time to go to the gym.

Deathbed regrets

Decision saturation

Delusions of SAHM grandeur

Demonic possession

Do not go gentle into that good night

Drive-thru kitchen

Dudley Do-Everything

Deathbed regrets: The list of failings that all mothers carry in their heads. For a working mother, the list may be governed by the fact that she spent too much of her kids' childhoods in the quiet comfort of her office. Each list is unique, and one that every mother probably has memorized, like her Social Security number. Depending on the woman, the items on her list may be things she keeps to herself, until she starts ranting about them on her deathbed.

A few of the items on my list:

- I have been a class mother only twice.
- I did not have a parent-teacher conference when my oldest son was in eighth grade because I lost the letter telling me when to schedule it.
- I have never volunteered in the elementary school lunchroom.
- I have never been on the PTA.

- I have never ironed my son's collection of achievement patches onto his soccer jacket.
- Once my children reach middle school, I can no longer remember their teachers' names.
- One year we lost my middle son's cello for three weeks, and it turned out it was at school the whole time. That's how often we made him bring it home to practice.
- I have never chaired a single school committee.
- Not one of my children has a baby book. (Someone should probably put me in jail for that.)

Decision saturation: The inevitable end-of-day point when you risk complete system shutdown if you are asked to focus for even one more minute. This may be when it's 8:45 p.m. and you are attempting to answer work e-mails or fill out the form for school lunch, or when your son is doing his homework and needs to know the ten events that have shaped him as a person—including exact dates if possible, and preferably accompanied by pictures. How can you remember the *exact* date that he got stitches above his eye or the first time he put on skis? And you certainly do not have a picture.

Delusions of SAHM grandeur: The phenomenon by which a working mom will actually believe that just because she is at home for a few days with the kids, it means she will be as talented/capable/patient/sane as her full-time stay-at-home-mom friends.

I have spent most of my fourteen-plus years as a working

mother maintaining the intermittent fantasy that I would rather be a stay-at-home mom. I also like to believe (this is where the delusion comes in) that I would be good at staying home—that is, until I am in Stop & Shop with three kids on New Year's Eve day and they insist on going through the self-checkout aisle, just to use one example. The slowness of the whole operation—not to mention the brothers who are kicking each other under the basket of the shopping cart over a slight that I didn't even detect—makes me feel like I just may have to blow my brains out. And whoever invented the self-checkout aisle should have to do some major community service.

There are quite a few problems with pretending to be a stay-at-home mom (a SAHM on training wheels, as it were) for short periods of time. First of all, your significant other is probably at work, so you're on your own, and you may not be accustomed to that. Second, there's just a lot of chaos that you're not accustomed to either. Third, it's much harder to be completely selfish when you've got little creatures milling around who have clear, immediate needs that you have to meet. Finally, you have spent your entire adult life learning to handle office politics, but none of those skills comes in handy when you enter the realm of domestic politics, which seems to be filled with children who regard fighting as some sort of spontaneous need, like the cast of *Mamma Mia!* when it spontaneously breaks into those disturbing ABBA songs. (See *Fight club,* p. 75.)

Oh, there are other, more mundane problems too. You go to the Gymboree class and you don't know the words to the parachute song or that your son needs a name tag, and this makes you feel like an interloper. You go to elementary school pickup and see clusters of women huddled together and you don't know where to stand, and this makes you feel like an impostor. You think you are being clever by putting the baby in the jogging stroller to walk a mile to the grocery store—fresh air for him, exercise for you!—to buy a big bag of clams for the clam chowder you think your older children will like, but by the time you get home and start cooking it's already 6:00 p.m., and the baby is hungry and tired and insists on being in your arms. If you were a full-time SAHM, you'd have some sort of clever kitchen drawer full of things just within your baby's reach to distract him while you try to figure out how to make clam chowder, which is much more labor-intensive than the recipe would suggest. But because you are a working mom, not only do you not have a clever drawer, but you don't know that you should have started dinner at 4:00, well before your two-year-old started freaking out and his older brothers began sullenly lurking around and asking when dinner would be ready without actually doing anything to help. And so you do the only thing that makes sense to you, which is to pour yourself a giant glass of wine and hope nobody notices. And start calling your husband every five minutes to find out when he's coming home. And take a long, hard look at the person you really are and admit: no, you do not have what it takes to be a good stay-at-home mom.

Demonic possession: Any mysterious, short-lived pain in your body that occurs during a period of acute domestic or career unhappiness. You think there is something seriously wrong with you, when actually an evil spirit has taken control of your physical being. If you work for a slave driver named Frank, for example, and you are experiencing stomach problems, you might just have a Frank in your small intestines. If your next-door neighbor Edith is giving you trouble and you wake up one morning feeling achy all over, you might have an Edith in your joints. Unfortunately, there is very little you can do. You are being inhabited, and you just have to wait for the evil spirit to leave you for someone else.

Do not go gentle into that good night: The antisleep oath children take the instant they emerge from the womb. This has a particularly negative effect on you when you have an early work meeting or want, for once this week, to make it to the gym in the morning. (See *Musical beds,* p. 142.)

Drive-thru kitchen: You get home from work at 6:30 and your husband has to run soccer practice at 7:00 and you have a library board meeting at 7:30. All members of the family, except those confined to a high chair, eat dinner in shifts, mostly standing up. Never your finest hour as a mother; makes you seriously wonder if you should blow up the family schedule and move to the middle of Alaska like Homer and Marge did in *The Simpsons Movie.*

Dudley Do-Everything: That rare creature who loves house-work, loves to manage kids' schedules, loves to cook, and wants to do everything he possibly can to help you find time to relax. In other words, the trophy husband.

As far as I can tell, Dudley Do-Everything husbands do exist, but you really have to go out of your way to find one, just like you have to go to the zoo if you ever want to see a polar bear. The fact of the matter is, the average husband — that is, the nontrophy variety — is just not bred to be terribly helpful, and the sooner a working woman realizes that her husband is of limited domestic use, the sooner she is going to have a happy marriage.

I grew up in a household of three daughters, and although I think the word *feminist* has lost its meaning, that's what we were groomed to be. I did my fair share of cooking and dusting and bathroom cleaning as a child, but the thought that I would spend my life with a husband who did not do a full 50 percent of the work involved in running a household never crossed my mind. It was not part of the dating screening process, I'll tell you that much. ("Um, you're really cute, but how do you feel about scheduling play dates?") And so I am married to a man who doesn't think it's at all unfair to turn to me on a Sunday afternoon and innocently ask, "What's for dinner?" On most Sundays, I will accept the question at face value and give him a simple answer. But on Sundays when I am feeling overwhelmed (see *Sunday night stomp,* p. 202), I will answer through clenched teeth while thinking to myself, *I don't know, honey. You tell me.*

In defense of my husband, he is excellent at a number of important household skills that I lack, many of which make him a wonderful parent. He is really good at sitting down and assembling a Brio train set; after fifteen minutes, I'm thinking, *How can I get out of this?* He is terrific at going out to the yard at the end of a long day and enthusiastically playing soccer with our boys; the whole experience makes me think, *Would anybody besides me care for a cocktail?* He knows the definition of nearly every word you can think of and can explain the Gilded Age/ electoral college/Pythagorean theorem to any curious eighth grader. (I, on the other hand, can tell you how much the house down the street is going on the market for and eight alternate uses for a Bounce dryer sheet.) He can play chess and speak French and knows the capital of all fifty states (I think—I'm not sure I could tell you if he was wrong). On the intelligence-compassion-interesting-person scale, he is off the charts, which is why I married him. But what the twenty-one-year-old me didn't realize when we met was that, in the long run, having read all of Shakespeare is not nearly as important as showing willingness—enthusiasm, in fact—when it comes to making breakfast for the children for two decades straight.

I often wonder what it would be like to have a trophy husband; I look at the very few men I know who fit that description and ponder the downside. I can think of one, and it's big: loss of control. If I were married to a man who bounded out of bed on a Saturday morning to make chocolate chip pancakes for the family—well, that would be sweet, but what if I wanted oatmeal? I waste no time in bitching about carrying the domestic burden, but there is something tremendously empowering about doing it all, because it means you are making most of the decisions. Would I really want to give up that level of control? I'm not sure. And so, much of my life as a wife and mother is about vacillating between wanting to do everything myself and being really, really mad that no one is helping me.

How do I train my own three boys to grow up to be helpful husbands? Every time I fold a clean pair of boxer shorts, am I just reinforcing the woman's role, signaling to them that aside from a period between high school and marriage they will never have to fold their own underwear for as long as they live? My boys have a short list of age-appropriate chores they have to do around the house, all tied to their weekly allowance (which every expert says is a no-no, for reasons I've never understood). Still, whenever they see Mom put on an apron while Dad is watching basketball, am I reinforcing expectations that their future wives or partners will resent? Should I get my husband an apron for his next birthday, just so he can put it on and give the illusion of cooking?

Because anger is the Marriage Killer, I try hard to readjust my impulses when my husband wants to know what's for dinner. After eighteen years of marriage, I have learned to ask for help, to make the family to-do list and give a good chunk of it to him. Things do not always get done my way or in my time frame, but I hope we are demonstrating to our three sons that yes, fathers take children to the orthodontist and do the grocery shopping. And, after these eighteen years of marriage, my definition of a trophy husband continues to evolve. Trophies come in all shapes and sizes, after all, and the secret is to be grateful for the one you've got.

E-mail — friend or foe?

Emotional intelligence

Emotional tourniquet

Everywoman's tale, or the story of your life

Existential lethargy

E-Z Pass to work-life happiness

E-mail—friend or foe? The question you constantly ask yourself with respect to this important tool that is both a key to flexibility and success . . . and an enormous ball and chain.

When I started out in the working world, there was no such thing as e-mail. Shocking, I realize, and yet we were still able to get quite a bit done. Now we all say we can't live without e-mail, but I would like to be first in line to try. E-mail is the kudzu of productivity: something that at first seems harmless and beneficial but that eventually takes over your entire world.

Perhaps the problem is not e-mail, but the coworkers who (mis)use it. Why do people send you e-mails and then call an hour later when they don't get a reply? Why do people think e-mail is more efficient, when answering a simple question sometimes takes hours of back and forth when it could be accomplished in a three-minute phone call? Why do publicists and people who work for you think it's OK to begin an e-mail with "Hey"? Why do people who write extremely long e-mails actually believe you will read to the bottom? Why does the "Reply to All" feature exist?

Obviously, there are benefits to e-mail that are tailored to working mothers like me. For example, I try not to look at my e-mail after I leave the office each day, because if I do, I will get sucked back into the work vortex and not hear a single thing anyone in my family says to me. Not to mention the fact that my children are relentless in their teasing if they catch me typing away on my BlackBerry when I think no one is looking. However, if I get up at 5:00 a.m. and need to communicate something to a coworker before I forget, e-mail is a beautiful thing. A good friend of mine was once advised by her husband that she should not send e-mails to her staff before 6:00 a.m., because it would just confirm their suspicions that she was a crazy workaholic. To that I say *pshaw*. If all the working moms I know had to stop predawn e-mailing, the business world would stop turning.

Emotional intelligence: A fundamental part of the grand human machine that, mysteriously, many people seem to lack. And yet they continue to function. Also called "E.Q.," for emotional intelligence quotient, not "E.I.," which would make a lot more sense.

There are so many stories we all have about people who demonstrate a perplexing absence of E.Q. in the workplace. I know a guy who would send e-mails to people who were nearly killing themselves on a project; the opening line would invariably be "What the fuck are you doing?" (Always effective in motivating a group.) I know a woman who, if she is working on her computer and an underling walks in, does not even turn around. She will have whole conversations without looking away from her screen. Head-scratchers, no?

To people like this, you want to say, "Did you skip kindergarten, or are you just an asshole?" Those of us who are not assholes and did not skip kindergarten know that we need to treat our fellow human beings with kindness and decency. One does not need to have heightened E.Q. to know this. I like to think that people who are missing E.Q. will eventually break down. How can they continue to function while missing a major part? Until then, they should all go sit in a corner and have a giant time-out.

Emotional tourniquet: The anti-tears device you must put on every day when you walk into work.

Make no mistake: crying is OK. Crying makes you feel better. I am the last person to advocate the abolishment of crying, seeing as I cry even when I watch bad, manipulative movies like *The Bodyguard* or *Click,* or hear cheesy love songs like that Celine Dion one from *Titanic.* But when you go in to work, you must check the tears at the door. I learned this lesson on one awful day, and now I will never forget it.

Because I believe I am inherently lucky (see *Leap of faith,* p. 125), I never anticipate the worst. For this reason I did not take my husband with me for the six-week sonogram appointment that revealed I had had a second miscarriage. Never mind that I knew from recent experience what it was like to lie in a dark room as a technician views your uterus in silence, waiting for the radiologist to deliver the bad news that there is no heartbeat. Because I believe I am inherently lucky, I did not imagine that the exact same thing would happen twice within a matter of months, and so I did not think that I would need my husband there to hold my hand as the radiologist confirmed what I could already see. Or once the appointment was over, to put his arms around me as I sobbed.

And so I left the radiologist's office and walked alone down Park Avenue, crying. I called my husband at the office and then cried harder. The day was overcast, and as I walked I imagined the clouds parting and God saying to me, "Kristin, I am trying to tell you something, but you are not listening to me. A third child is a bad idea. You have a wonderful life. Stop trying to mess it up."

Part of my wonderful life was my job, working with a wonderful team, including a new creative director who had moved all the way from Australia to join our staff. That was her first day of work, and I had planned to throw a breakfast party to welcome her to the magazine as soon as I got to the office. But there I was, crying on Park Avenue. I didn't know what to do. About eight blocks from my office I found a little park and sat down on a low wall. There was no bright side, no pep-talking myself out of this. I decided to do the one thing that seemed possible, which was to imagine putting my heart in a box and taping that box shut. I would go to work and throw the party and give a bright little speech to welcome the creative director, and no one would know what was in the box because it would remain tightly shut until I got home that night. And I did it, and it worked.

I realize this is an extreme example. It's not every day that one of the saddest things that has ever happened to you occurs on the morning that you have to throw a party. But it taught me that I can control the crying, I can apply that emotional tourniquet, I can put on a happy face when I am dying inside. It was a great lesson, one that everyone should know. And I hope I never have to apply it again.

Everywoman's tale, or the story of your life: The fact that your path through the mystery and wonder that adulthood once seemed to offer has led you straight to an extremely average existence, which is strangely satisfying.

There are all sorts of ways people define reaching maturity: when you have kids of your own; when you abandon childhood dreams; when you spot your first gray hair or begin to think a little eye lift might not be such a bad idea after all. I submit that you reach maturity when you realize that, despite everything your parents have told you over the years, you really are fundamentally just average. And that is — shockingly — OK.

I cannot claim to be mature, but I will say that I realized

I was fundamentally average when we moved to the suburbs and it was one of the best days of my life. At the age of twenty-four I started out life in New York on the Upper West Side of Manhattan, pursuing an urban fantasy created by people like Woody Allen and Nora Ephron. I lived down the block from Central Park, which was delightful. There was a stable on my street, so every day I'd hear the *clip-clop* of horses making their way home. Horses walking down my New York City street! Magic! But then I encountered the sneaker problem. That is: in Manhattan it is never acceptable for a sophisticated adult who is not a model or an actress to wear sneakers, unless she is about to go for a jog. Because I spend my weekdays in high heels, I really do like a good sneaker on the weekend. And so I moved to Brooklyn.

In Brooklyn you could wear sneakers, and you could have children. In Manhattan you could have children too, but you either had to be a gazillionaire or pay a special fine. In Brooklyn you could be a normal person of average means and have a baby, which I did. But about the time our first son turned one, our formerly charming brownstone apartment was overrun with plastic toys that nannies would trip over (see *Heartbreak by babysitter,* p. 90) and that flew out of any closet door you dared to crack open. Plus we had a car, a hand-me-down from my in-laws that we parked on the street. But because of street-cleaning regulations, the car constantly had to be moved to avoid being ticketed. For some reason this moving always seemed to happen at 11:00 at night and require a good half hour of driving around looking for a free spot, which was enough to make you want to burn your driver's license. And so we moved to the suburbs.

Fictional representations of the suburbs are all about people who are either crazy (*Desperate Housewives, American Beauty*), fairly boring or unbelievably stupid (*Home Improvement, The Simpsons*), or depressed and possibly about to kill themselves (*Revolutionary Road, The Ice Storm, Far from Heaven*, etc., etc., etc.). Where are the movies about suburbanites who are normal, interesting, and of above-average intelligence? I know these people exist; I am surrounded by them. Which is not to say that morons and lunatics do not exist in the suburbs; just spend a day on the sidelines of a suburban soccer field and you witness adult behavior that will make your toes curl. But for the most part the suburbs are populated by the same people who live in the city, except they own hedge trimmers and are 3 percent happier because they don't have to worry about alternate-side-of-the-street parking.

When we first moved to the suburbs and people at work asked me where I lived, I would say "the unmentionables," or I'd whisper the name of my town and stare at my feet. There is no doubt that living in the suburbs is a marker of bourgeois desires, a suggestion that you are living the unexamined life and prefer it that way. At least that's true for those in my profession. But after thirteen years, I'm unapologetic enough about my choice that I actually feel a bit superior to most city dwellers of the nongazillionaire variety. As it turns out, my husband and I have fairly pedestrian needs: a bed big enough to accommodate two tallish adults and occasional visiting children; a dog to greet us at the door at the end of a long day; a neighborhood safe enough that if we drive home from vacation late at night we can leave our luggage in the car until the morning—in our own driveway!—without fear of a break-in; a little yard where my kids can deposit soccer balls and lacrosse sticks and baseball bats and never have to worry about retrieving them unless forced to by one of their parents (which doesn't happen as often as it should). The suburbs can offer us these things without tremendous stress or effort; the city cannot. Hence my vague superiority: I am able to meet the pedestrian needs of my pedestrian family, all without spending four million dollars or charming a co-op board.

Then there is the matter of the commute, which is shorter from our suburb to midtown Manhattan than it was from Brooklyn. When my husband and I first started looking to leave the city, we focused on a bucolic town that would have meant an hour-long train ride. I loved the place and found it much more charming than where we finally settled, but all I could think was: What if someone falls off the monkey bars on the playground and breaks his collarbone? I would go crazy sitting on Metro-North for a full hour, trying to rush home to my child. And so we chose a town that is only a half-hour train ride from midtown. I have easy access to both breakfast meetings in the city and parent-teacher conferences at home: equally necessary in my current life. Of course, having to make a certain train at an exact time of day to be at a work meeting or to relieve our babysitter adds so much stress to my existence that it's already shortened my life span by about seven years (see

Stress fracture, p. 200). But compared to the stress of alternate-side-of-the-street parking, that's nothing.

Existential lethargy: The state you're trapped in when you're so overwhelmed that nothing — and I mean nothing — interests you, not even Starbucks or a York Peppermint Pattie. This state is particularly acute at the beginning of the school year, the end of the school year, any time from November 23 to January 2, and on Halloween.

E-Z Pass to work-life happiness: Any clever device you employ to maintain your sanity while attempting to function at a high level both at the office and at home.

A few things that have worked for me:

- Leave the office at the same time every day, preferably 5:30. This is a necessity, like jury duty. Do not allow anyone to question this habit.
- Exercise three days a week and don't expect any more of yourself in the physical-fitness department.
- Make your kids walk the dog.
- Ask your husband to be in charge of everything related to kids' sports. Kids' sports are the second most time-consuming thing about being a parent, after laundry.
- Find one great teacher gift and stick to it year after year (you can never go wrong with a Barnes & Noble gift certificate).

- Choose the best child care you can possibly afford, even if it's a stretch. When your friends who scrimp on child care tell you that you're crazy, secretly roll your eyes, remain silent, and think of all the ways in which your children are superior to theirs.

Family-friendly living
Fight club
First, do no harm
Flamethrower e-mail
Flipping your appearance
Friends with benefits
From here to eternity
Full hard drive
Full stop

Family-friendly living: The happy-sad reality that your family is actually much, much better off because you work. And we're not just talking about the money.

A few months back I had lunch with my friend Janet, a fellow editor and working mom who has been successful for most of her life. She is witty, engaging, smart, opinionated, bossy — all things that make her both a great editor and a terrific lunch date. We had not seen each other for a while and had quite a bit to catch up on, much of it having to do with how Janet had been spending her days as a consultant since she had — for the first time in her life — lost her office job some nine months before.

After lunch we walked toward my office and got to talking about her kids. Janet has a daughter in high school and a son who recently graduated from college, both of whom seem happy, intelligent, and well adjusted: the working mom's hat trick. I told her she must be pleased with the way her children turned out. "Well," she said, "it's mostly because I wasn't around to screw them up."

Apparently Janet had realized—especially now that she had more time to send her daughter off to school in the morning and welcome her home in the afternoon, not to mention focus on things like lost books and sports schedules and what was for lunch—that if she had been more involved in the minutiae of her children's lives, they might not have turned out so happy, intelligent, or well adjusted. In short, Janet's career was enough of a distraction that she was actually able to be a pretty good mother. Now that she wasn't working full-time, Janet no longer knew who she was, and things were threatening to go off the rails.

Although each of my children has, on occasion, asked me why I work and some other mothers don't, none of them has ever requested that I actually stop. There is a tacit understanding between me and the rest of my family that we all benefit with me out of the house. My children know that I am hyperactive, and stomp around if I've had too much coffee, and attach entirely too much importance to silly things like the fact that there are always dirty socks on the floor of every single room of our house. But they also know that when I am stomping around and going on about dirty socks, or the fact that our oldest son must listen to loud music while he does his homework, or that our middle son insists on bouncing balls off every hard surface in the kitchen, they just have to ride out the storm because soon enough I will go to work and stop bugging them. Heaven forbid I stick around long enough to focus on the sock situation, for example, because all sorts of bad habits would then be uncovered, like the fact that my children go through four different pairs of socks every single day, one after another like they were paper napkins. My sons and I know that we are all better off with Mom in the safety of her padded office and them in the care of a babysitter who is loving, friendly, intelligent, and efficient, and who knows that socks are just socks.

If I stayed at home, things would not be pretty (see *Delusions of SAHM grandeur,* p. 52). The baby would be a biter and the eldest would get stoned every day before school. Our middle son — who, unlucky devil, is the most like me of our three kids — would have killed me by now, or vice versa, and so he would either be dead or in some sort of awful juvenile correctional facility. And everybody would miss him, because he is the funniest one among us. (Really — our little family voted last summer, and he won. I didn't get a single vote.) As much as I fantasize from time to time about getting off the hamster wheel of commuting and office politics and all the other stress-inducing, soul-crushing things that make working so…unpleasant, I know that that is where I belong, for my own health and the health of my family. And for every person who then wonders, *So why did you have children in the first place, lady?* there is a Janet, who knows that some of the most functional families involve parents and children who see one another mostly on nights and weekends. And everybody is happier for it.

Fight club: The secret society your children belong to that requires them to spontaneously pinch, punch, or otherwise provoke one another whenever you are in a hurry to get out of the house. Usually someone ends up on the floor and needs the (lost or, if found, out of tape) lint roller to get the dog hair off, among many other irritating delays.

First, do no harm: What you must constantly remind yourself when you're tempted to kill one of your children.

Second, tell your child that if he is not at the front door with his backpack in five minutes, he will not play Guitar Hero for five days.

Third, consider whether you can put mascara on in the car without injury or extreme embarrassment. (Probably not.)

Fourth, take a really deep breath. No, you are not as organized as you might be. Yes, your children are rarely on time for school. But they are sweet kids who make you laugh and who are unfailingly polite, at least to people who are not their parents. Which reminds you: *Why* do you have to ask your son eight times to put on his sneakers?!? Does his teacher have to ask even more than once or twice?

Fifth, take another deep breath; see step one.

Flamethrower e-mail: The incendiary message you don't expect that promptly ruins an otherwise lovely day. The e-mail may be from a boss, an annoying coworker, a difficult friend, a teenage daughter. Regardless of who sends it, suddenly your whole world is on fire.

Flipping your appearance: A quick fix to make up for years of deferred maintenance. Flipping is especially helpful and confidence building before holidays, school or family reunions, important work trips, and beach vacations. Effective flipping techniques include getting a half head of highlights, buying Spanx tights, putting on a pair of heels that are half an inch higher than is actually comfortable, paying to have your clothes tailored so they look more expensive than they are, and the careful application of self-tanner. Note: Where cellulite on the back of your thighs is concerned, there is no flipping strategy that works. Alas.

Friends with benefits:
- Will pick your child up from school when your babysitter is sick: 5 points
- Will go out of her way to fill you in on school gossip that you may have missed: 3 points
- Will actually listen patiently to your boring work complaints and be more sympathetic than your husband: 2 points
- Will not be offended when you are too busy to socialize: 8 points
- Will take your toddler to the bathroom to change his poopy diaper so you can watch your older child's band concert: 300 points

From here to eternity: The terrible sinking feeling you have when you are no longer interested in your current job but can't see a way out of it or, worse, figure out what you'd rather do instead. If you are prone to drama and exaggeration when the chips are down, you imagine spending the rest of your life in that same office or cubicle, until you eventually die of boredom.

Also applies to the mind-numbing panic you feel when you think you just cannot watch that Elmo DVD one more time, but it's the only thing that sufficiently occupies your toddler so you can get ready for work in the morning. Will you still be watching Elmo when he's thirteen?

Full hard drive: The state you've reached when you can't take in any more information, so when your husband tells you that one of his sports activities has changed from Wednesday morning to Wednesday night, you will simply never, ever remember this because there is no room to store it. You can try to delete other items, but it's too late.

Full stop: Those relatively rare times when the whirling dervish (you) halts all movement. My full stops come when:

- A child has a high fever.
- A coworker cries in my office.
- A key member of my team resigns.
- A child throws up.
- I receive really bad news about my competition.
- I receive really good news about my competition.
- The school secretary or camp nurse calls, even if she begins the conversation with "Everything is fine."

Note: full-stop moments are vital to life in general and your well-being in particular, as reminders that much of what you think is important actually isn't, in the grand scheme of things.

Getting to yes
Glass ceiling
Good cop / bad cop
Good-enough fill-in-the-blank
Guilt curve

Getting to yes: Those magical moments when you ask someone to do something and he doesn't say "But..."

Glass ceiling: From what I hear, the thing that prevents women in the workplace from rising beyond a certain level, or some such. Apparently, working mothers everywhere are absolutely obsessed with the glass ceiling; I just don't happen to know any of them. The working moms I know are mostly worried about who is going to take out the trash.

Which is not to say there aren't a few analogous worries in the lives of my working-mom friends. They are:

- "Glass pile of crap": when you leave a bunch of stuff at the bottom of the stairs, clearly meant to be taken to the second floor by any thinking adult who sees it, why does your husband just walk by it instead of picking everything up?

- "Glass paunch": why is it acceptable for a man over the age of fifty to have a little belly, when on a woman over fifty it just means she's lazy or really likes the sauce?
- "Glass sex life": if you fall asleep every night before your husband comes to bed, is he eventually going to have an affair?
- "Glass forced retirement": once you reach the age when everyone you work with is younger than you are, is it time to go?
- "Glass Lothario": if good-looking thirty-something men no longer give you a second glance — if, in fact, they try to look right through you to see if there is a cuter, younger woman with firmer breasts standing behind you — is it time for plastic surgery?

Good cop/bad cop: The two sides of your personality that you ably control and employ as needed, sometimes concurrently.

Say you are in a work meeting and your son calls, first on your office line, then on your cell phone, then on your office line again. You pick up, in case someone is in the emergency room. "I'm so sorry," you say to your coworkers. (Good cop.)

Your son desperately wants to have a sleepover that night, even though he already has a sleepover planned for the following night and soccer practice at 8:00 a.m. *"Absolutely not,"* you say in your conversation-ending voice. (Bad cop.)

Back to the coworkers, with a smile. "Where were we?" (Good cop.)

Good-enough fill-in-the-blank: The understanding that what you are striving for most of the time in life need not be the A+ you were taught to want in school, but merely a passing grade. There are hundreds of work and home situations in which you absolutely don't need to aim any higher than good enough, and they include: pasta, enforcement of rules, entertaining, ironing, appearance maintenance, bathroom cleaning, premeeting preparation, PowerPoint presentations, e-mail vigilance, desk neatness, chocolate chip cookies.

Guilt curve: The process by which your feelings of shame and inadequacy about being a working mom grow and then diminish. In my experience, the guilt curve is a bell curve, peaking when your first child reaches kindergarten, with a long tail that lasts until the day of your funeral.

My husband and I waited until we were married for four years before having our first child. During that time I worked, naturally; what else was I supposed to do? I had a fine education and lots of energy and a strong work ethic instilled in me by two hardworking parents who had spent decades telling me that I could accomplish anything I set out to do. Not to mention the fact that I was living in New York City and had a lot of rent to pay.

After our first son was born I continued to work because that niggling rent situation just wouldn't go away. I also happened to love my job, but that did not erase the fact that I was leaving my son every day with a woman I hardly knew. I was not sewing adorable curtains for the nursery or spending long hours breast-feeding on the sofa or even hanging out at the playground — all the things I imagined a good mother did. Thus the guilt.

There is nothing more effective in mitigating guilt than knowing that half your friends are making the same "mistake." Most of the other mothers I knew then also worked, which helped. The fact that I had no role model did *not* help; my mother hadn't worked until my youngest sister was in high school, and just about every female boss I had ever had was not someone I wanted to grow up to be (see *Role model reversal,* p. 185). But my job continued to get more interesting and my rent turned into an even bigger mortgage payment. Most important, my children actually seemed fine. Astonishing.

And so my children and I grew, with guilt shadowing us. Sometimes guilt looks like the fantasy you once had about your future and sometimes it looks like the ghost of the family that you are not. Sometimes it's a dull hum in the background; sometimes it's a giant rock that falls on your head. But it continues to change as you change and, unless you are irredeemably neurotic, it gets smaller as you get wiser.

Along the way there are setbacks: distinct moments on your guilt curve that confirm that you have made all the wrong choices and probably never should have had children in the first place. Maybe no one else remembers these moments, but you certainly do. For example: the day before Easter 2000, I was at the Shoe Boat in the Concord Mall in Wilmington, Delaware, buying new sneakers for my six-year-old son. I have never been a great mother where shoes are concerned because I just can't seem to remember that feet continue to grow. That morning at the Shoe Boat, the helpful (seeming) gentleman who worked there measured my son's foot and announced that it was two sizes bigger than the shoes I had been wedging his feet into for the past who knows how many months. "Bad mommy!" he exclaimed. Everybody laughed, except me. Of course, the reason I remember this incident so clearly is that it became honed in my mind into a fine, hard guilt-thorn that poked me in the side every time I thought my life as a working mom was progressing smoothly. And if you had all the time in the world I could give you about three hundred other incidents just like that one.

But there are also moments along the curve—these come later—when you realize that everything is pretty much OK, that you have managed to produce both a decent career and fairly well-adjusted children who miraculously don't hate you. Four years after that Saturday in the Shoe Boat I was driving in the car with my two sons, then aged ten and seven, and my younger guy was asking for the eightieth time that week why he was not permitted to do something that his older brother could do. "Because," I said, exasperated, "he's in fifth grade, and you're in third grade!"

"Mom!" he said. "I'm in *second* grade!"

This time when everybody laughed, I laughed too. Because I was far enough along on my curve that guilt had changed from the sharp thorn to a worn little nub that I could still feel but that no longer really hurt. I was finally evolved enough to know that just because I temporarily forgot what grade my son was in did not mean that I forgot his birth weight, the fact that he likes his pasta with meatballs and cheese but no sauce, or that *Yes Man* is his favorite movie. Or how much I love him.

Hamster wheeling
"Having it all"
Hearing aid
Heartbreak by babysitter
Homeward bound
Human Whack-a-Mole
Humor index

Hamster wheeling: The depressing state of being when you feel like you're running around and around but not actually getting anyplace or accomplishing anything. This can happen at home (arguing with a spouse or a child) or at work (having the same meeting over and over again until your patience, imagination, and love of fellow man run out).

"Having it all": The phrase you occasionally hear to describe some sort of magical state in which a working mother has reached the Xanadu of modern womanhood.

There have been times when people have told me that I "have it all." I am not quite sure how to respond to this. Indeed, I am tremendously blessed with healthy children, a house I like, a husband who suits me, and a job that does not drive me bananas.

There is no woman, however, who has it all. Aside from the very obvious sacrifices we all make in the tug-of-war that is working and managing a family, we all have an evolving list of things we lack. Here are just a few things I would need in my life to be able to say that I "have it all":

- More sleep
- Fewer piles of miscellaneous things that need to be put away on the top of my dresser, on the bench in our bedroom, on the floor at the foot of the bench—in fact, everywhere I look
- Coworkers who never use "Reply to All"
- Better hair
- A cat who did not throw up in odd, unpredictable spots throughout the house

Perhaps someday I will have these things. Then when someone says to me, "You certainly have it all," I will look her in the eye and say, "Thank you! I guess I do."

Hearing aid: The realization—after years on the job and as a parent spent trying to solve every problem that comes your way—that a lot of the time people just want to be heard. The beleaguered coworker just wants to vent; she's not asking you to change her life. And the tired child merely wants to complain at the end of the day but doesn't really expect you to know why other kids can be such jerks.

Heartbreak by babysitter: The unique, surprising loss you experience when the person who has been watching over your children exits your little world, even if you have forced that exit.

In my life as a working mother I have always employed full-time babysitters to care for my children. In the Greater New York area, this is a common practice; it is a luxury, but one that many working parents can afford. There are countless advantages to having someone take care of your children in your own house, and I can't imagine doing it any other way. But there are also, inevitably, the breakups.

In fourteen years I have broken up with three babysitters. The first one was named Judy. Judy was a tall, quiet woman, and at this point I don't remember a whole lot about her except that she took care of our oldest son for the first sixteen months of his life. She was a good introduction to the drama that can accompany a babysitter: in the course of a year she got pregnant, fell on a toy in our living room (so she said) and sprained her shoulder, and went into labor in our apartment. We parted ways with Judy when we moved to the suburbs, and I did not cry when we broke up.

Then came Juliet, who was with our family for five years. Juliet is an amazing woman: she immigrated to this country as an adult, raised two fine children on her own, and put herself and her daughter through college. Juliet represented level two of babysitter drama: during those five years, she had several gallbladder attacks and then gallbladder surgery, learned to drive (after twice failing the test), and got pregnant and took maternity leave. She is a tough cookie; anyone over the age of twenty is guilty until proven innocent in Juliet's view and therefore must be treated with extreme suspicion. Adults in particular are to be disliked at first sight. Juliet has such a gruff, unaccommodating demeanor that one mother cornered me in the nursery school parking lot and informed me that my babysitter was "a psychopath." But to me Juliet was like a turtle: extremely hard on the outside, all softness underneath. And my kids loved her.

Once our oldest was in second grade, though, we needed someone who could drive on the highway, help with homework, and send an e-mail. And maybe, just maybe, someone who was a little... friendlier. At the same time, Juliet wanted to cut back on her hours so she could work toward her undergraduate degree. So we said good-bye, and we both cried. But just a bit.

Then we hired Lauren. Lauren was with us for seven years. She was newly divorced when we hired her, and in seven years she got married and divorced again; developed a gluten allergy; had knee surgery, pneumonia, and a pregnancy. (That's right: three babysitters, three pregnancies. What are the odds?) During that time, we produced some sizeable life changes of our own: a new dog, a new house, a new baby, a new kitchen. And, for the boys: the beginning of nursery school, elementary school, and middle school; first big-boy underpants, first cavity filled, first girlfriend. Every time we threw her a curveball (we're moving! I'm pregnant!), she hit it out of the park. She was capable in nearly every way: she could buzz-cut hair, make chicken parmigiana from memory, program the car radio, load the cat into his carrier (nearly impossible), and figure out how to get photos from the digital camera to the computer to a disc to CVS for printing. She was friendly and energetic and laughed all the time and the kids thought she was absolutely perfect.

And still. Seven years is a long time. By the end we both needed a change: she wanted more flexibility just as our schedule grew more demanding. When we officially broke up, we cried. Then we laughed, and cried again. When I later informed our children, I actually sobbed, which I don't do very often and certainly not in front of them.

To this day I can't figure out why I cried so hard. Didn't I want that change? Wasn't I ready for something else? All I can think is that Lauren broke my heart. She broke my heart because she understood my kids nearly as well as I did. And sometimes, when I was being Psycho Mom about something unimportant (like the fact that my teenage son never wears a winter coat) and she was just letting it roll off her back — well, then I think she understood them even more.

Part of what makes heartbreak so painful is that someone is showing you something about yourself that you don't really want to see. There are a number of unappealing parts of my personality that Lauren (unintentionally) revealed: I'm too high-strung, I'm too rushed, half the time I'm not really listening. The fact that the tumbleweeds of dog hair in our kitchen can ruin my mood does not say good things about my maturity level or ability to put things in perspective. I am compassionate, but when, for example, you know you have a gluten allergy and you eat a piece of regular bread anyway and then are too sick to show up for work ... well, by the third time this happens my compassion runs out. Shouldn't compassion be limitless? (Perhaps not when it's combined with a complicated salary arrangement, unlimited use of our car, and partial ownership of my children's hearts.)

One final thing the Lauren breakup revealed: although I am now well into my second decade of babysitter-mom arrangements, I cannot say I'm getting any wiser about the relationship. I'm getting smarter about handling sick days and maternity leaves and Christmas bonuses and paid overtime, but when it comes to understanding the emotional ties I have with the woman who mothers my children while I'm at work, I just seem to be getting dumber all the time. We are now nearly a year into our relationship with our fourth babysitter, Christina. She is like a ray of sunshine every day she enters our house at 8:00 a.m. So far, things are going very well, and I have high hopes. As always.

Homeward bound: The powerful drive you feel to get back into your house at the end of the day. The drive is so powerful, in fact, that sometimes it makes you do things that are irrational or completely out of character.

Like when my calm, loving friend Silvia was being driven home from the train station by her (calm, loving) teenage son, after a long, hard day at her demanding job. They were mere blocks from home when her son rear-ended the car in front of them at a stop sign. Before she could even think, Silvia turned to her son and said, "Are you *fucking kidding me?*"

Human Whack-a-Mole: An infuriating phenomenon demonstrated by unruly children and unmanageable colleagues. It goes like this: when you try to correct one behavior with a good whack, the person in question acts out in some other way. Husbands are not exempt. Say your husband spends too much time playing golf. You complain, he cuts back on golf, the problem disappears. You breathe a sigh of relief, and the next thing you know, a men's indoor soccer league has popped up on the family calendar.

Humor index: The scale by which you can measure all coworkers to determine how much you want to integrate them into your nonwork life.

0–1: No discernible sense of humor whatsoever. If you don't even say hello to this person when you pass in the hall, it probably doesn't matter (unless she is your boss).

2–3: Marginal. Exercise caution before so much as inviting her to lunch.

4–5: Shows promise. Very good for lunch and occasional after-work drinks. When your kids visit the office, you take them to see her, and she just may have something fun in an office drawer.

6–7: Potential lifelong friend. Invite her to dinner at your house; see if she brings an odd gift or there are awkward silences. If so, do not proceed beyond this level.

8–9: Truly a good friend. Go straight to her office if you feel like you are going to cry; before you resign, tell her first.

10: Soul mate. You work in the same industry and have everything in common. If you have any more children, name one after her.

Ignore the tray
Image consultant
It takes a village

Ignore the tray: The advice generally reserved for waiters that can apply to working mothers as well. That is, if you focus too much on the load you are carrying — for example, if you look too closely at next week's schedule, factoring in work- and child-related commitments — it will tip. Chin up, chest out, watch where you're headed, everything will be just fine.

Image consultant: An individual who shapes the persona that you present to the world, whether you like that persona or not.

Last winter I found myself in a medical clinic at the bottom of a mountain, staring at an X-ray of my father's arm. He had fallen while skiing the day before, and my youngest son and I accompanied him on a visit to the doctor. My father, Piet, insisted that his wrist was only sprained, but the X-ray told a different story. Dad sat in the examining room while the doctor and I looked at the film on the light box in the hall. "Well," the doctor said solemnly, "I see an abnormality here."

"Doctor," I replied, "you have *no idea*." I said this because, ever the dutiful daughter, I was following one of Piet van Ogtrop's Rules for Living; in this case, number 28: "Always try to charm a stranger by getting him to laugh." This particular stranger did not laugh, however, so I moved directly to rule number 19: "Know your audience, and modify your behavior accordingly." I dropped the humor and became serious like the doctor, *stat,* which seemed to improve matters. We promptly got Dad's arm wrapped up and left the clinic, but not before the doctor and half the staff learned, from Dad, how old I was when I gave birth to my youngest—nearly forty-three!—and what I did for a living—edit a big magazine in New York City! (Rule number 367: "Never hesitate to tell anybody the most mundane details about yourself or your family, because there is always the outside chance that they might be slightly interested.") For my part, I shared that Dad had broken his wrist because he was trying to keep up with his sons-in-law, who, after all, were thirty years younger; and did he mention that he shattered his elbow when he fell off a ladder while cleaning the gutters the day after Thanksgiving, in the rain?

I never set out to be so much like my father, and I think it's safe to say that neither of my sisters did either. But somehow Piet van Ogtrop's Rules for Living became a sort of guiding force, and we've all grown up into our own versions of our idio-syncratic, lovable, stubborn dad, both at home and at work.

When my sister Valerie was a child, her favorite activity was cleaning her room. (Rule number 48: "Clutter must be avoided at all costs.") Now she is a grown-up, and it's still her favorite activity. Being in Valerie's house is like being in a fancy hotel, except it's smaller and the bedspreads aren't filled with germs. I am always a little depressed when I leave her house to return to mine because, among other things, she is living proof that "a place for everything and everything in its place" can indeed have practical application in the real world, if you just focus.

Valerie was a math major in college, which is a very tidy line of study (there is always an answer), as opposed to a muddy one like English, my major (where everything is open to interpretation). For a time Valerie was an actuary, which I can hardly spell, much less explain. Now she works as the head of planning and distribution for a big retailer; it's a job where three of her major personality traits (she's bossy, she loves clothes, and she's really good at math) all come together in one successful package. She has two boys who are a lot of fun to be around, and not just because they always remember to take their shoes off at the door.

When my sister Claire was a child, her favorite activity was updating the lists that shaped her life. The first time she met my future husband, she demanded a list of his favorite bands, and for years she kept an ever-changing list of favorite names for her future children. (Rule number 8: "Start with a list!") They were all names that had a vague *Masterpiece Theatre* feel (Astrid, Eugenia), and, although she now has three children, I don't think she ever used a name from the list. But she has maintained her interest in organization, lists, and humanity in general, and for reasons I can't explain she remembers friends of mine that I have long since forgotten. Which — when she asks me how so-and-so is doing, and I don't even remember who so-and-so is—makes me feel like a bad person.

As a clinical social worker, Claire now spends her week exercising a patience in relating to her fellow man that I could not muster if you denied me caffeine for three months and removed half my brain. She lives by the *Diagnostic and Statistical Manual of Mental Disorders,* which is just an enormous, organized list of all the many things that could be wrong with you, and probably are. She also homeschools her children, raises chickens, makes pies from berries she picks by the side of the road, and grows things from seed. In short, nearly everything Claire does requires organization (and extreme determination, but that's another story).

Genetic material aside, maybe we have grown up unconsciously following Dad's rules because we lived in a family that was secretly patriarchal, even though Helen Reddy's "I Am Woman" was practically our theme song when we were kids. Or maybe it's because Mom didn't work until we were older, and our only working role model was Dad. We all grew up to be working women. It's not like our parents encouraged that, but they did encourage us to marry for love, and you know how that goes.

Our mother, Connie, had her own set of rules. A stay-at-home mom who went back to graduate school when Claire was in grade school, Mom spent most of my childhood sewing clothes, curtains, and slipcovers; growing vegetables; arranging flowers; watching sports competitions (field hockey, volleyball, swimming, diving, track, tennis); caring for pets;

washing and folding thousands of loads of laundry; and rinsing, chopping, mincing, dicing, sautéing, boiling, frying, braising, roasting, and baking. Not to mention canning and freezing. Our mother was, and continues to be, very *active* and *achievement oriented,* and many of her rules reflected that. A sample:

- Reading a novel during the day is acceptable only if you are a child or bedridden adult, and you'd better be pretty sick.
- Trying to carry too many bags of groceries from the car at once is a "lazy man's load" and you are a superior person if you make more trips.
- No TV until the evening news, period. If you watch soap operas after school like half your friends, you will never amount to anything. (If I died tomorrow my headstone would read: "Devoted Wife and Mother, Never Watched *General Hospital.*")

Back to my father and the doctor. After our field trip to the clinic, we headed home, where I took advantage of my son's nap time to do some work (rule number 17: "Idleness is misery"). Dad hung around, cheerful as always, muttering (rule number 340: "Talking to yourself is perfectly OK, and can sometimes be very productive") about whether to unwrap and rewrap his arm (rule number 266: "No offense, but I probably know more than you do"). The next day he did and, I have to admit, he did a pretty decent job.

It takes a village: The nifty if unrealistic notion that we can all just band together to attain the unattainable when it comes to the care of our children.

I don't know about you, but I could certainly use a village for the following:

- To find all pieces of a boy's lacrosse uniform, including helmet, mouth guard, and cup, and help the boy get dressed
- To outfit my children for any dressy occasion, as there appears to be a creature who eats khakis living in our attic
- To convince my husband that four sports for one child in one season is about three sports too many
- To get my middle son to eat anything in less than half an hour
- To show my husband how to empty and refill the Diaper Genie
- To convince my oldest son that when you brush the dog right outside the door, all the hair will blow back into the house, which defeats the purpose
- To keep our two-year-old as sweet as he is right now — forever

Jerry-rigged control
Juggler's lament
Jury of your peers
Just between us
"Just let me lie down"
Just a second
"Just very ambitious"

Jerry-rigged control: The only way you can succeed in your daily struggle to maintain sanity while surrounded by events and individuals who conspire against you. Your effort to "keep it all together" and "stay on top of things" demands nonstop improvisation and vigilance, which leads annoyed family members to make observations like "You are so controlling." In a loving way, of course.

Not too long ago I found myself in the middle of a conversation with a (smart, empathetic) child psychologist who informed me that I should not be telling my eleven-year-old son to brush his teeth. Instead, I should say to him, "Do you want to brush your teeth?"

I stared at her, speechless.

"Why don't you say, 'Do you want to brush your teeth?'" she repeated.

"Because," I said, "his answer will be, 'No, I don't.'"

"Well," she said patiently, "then you say to him, 'Do you want to keep the teeth you have?'"

By this point she had lost me. She seemed like a very nice woman so I just nodded and smiled, instead of telling her what was in the thought bubble over my head, which was that I don't have fifteen minutes every morning to *discuss* dental health with my eleven-year-old, especially when we are late for school. It's just that much more, shall we say, efficient, to yell, "Go brush your teeth! Right now!"

Immediately after this conversation with the psychologist, I e-mailed my sister Valerie. "News flash," I wrote. "It appears I am too controlling." I could practically hear her hooting as she read the message, even though she lives in the next state. "Ridiculous," she e-mailed back. "I am the controlling one in the family. You are not controlling." She then went on to point out that if she were not controlling, her children would:

- Not have school clothes
- Not arrive at birthday parties with presents
- Not eat vegetables or drink milk
- Be allowed to watch the movie *Shooter* every weekend starting at age four

Now, the child psychologist might submit that part of the reason I love and rely on Valerie so much is because she is an *enabler* when it comes to what some people might regard as my controlling behavior. Maybe in fact the only reason I have "loved" my sister as much as I have for these forty-some years is because she is more controlling than I am and therefore makes me feel better about myself. But really, who cares?

My husband does not quite see me as my sister does, but for the most part he silently endures the controlling aspects of my nature; after all, there's something in it for him. (As in: my insistence that the children actually eat a decent breakfast under my watchful eye means that my husband gets to stay out of the kitchen entirely and watch *SportsCenter* on ESPN nearly every single morning of the week.) However, I do worry that someday he's going to get together with my brothers-in-law and write a book: *Controlling Women and the Men Who (Used to) Love Them.* It's not all wine and roses when you live with a woman who is accustomed to telling people what to do. Sometimes my husband complains that because I spend my days bossing people around at work — where I am actually paid to do that and regularly get results — I (annoyingly, incorrectly) assume that such bossy behavior will work just as well at home.

But why don't bossiness and controlling behavior work well at home? Why don't the members of your family ever feel grateful when you take the painful decision-making process out of their hands? It certainly can work in the office, where everybody knows that sometimes people just want you to make decisions for them. It doesn't matter whether it's a good decision or a bad one, or whether they agree with you or not; it's a Decision. And then no matter what happens, everyone else can look you in the face and say, "It's not my fault."

Currently the most popular complaint in my house is "Mom is so controlling." I honestly don't think my kids know what this means, although it sounds good, especially when you are fourteen and can accompany it with an eye roll. This statement does not hurt my feelings, no matter how often they say it, although I do think it has a negative effect on me. If expressed too often, "Mom is so controlling" leads me to the I-told-you-so place where I actually start wondering how they would possibly manage if I kicked the bucket. If I'm dead, then no one will remember to get the cat's medication or realize that the houseplants do need water to live or know to buy end-of-year gifts for the teachers or factor in an extra five minutes to get out of the house when our middle son has just bought new sneakers, because it's going to take him that much longer to figure out how to get them on without actually untying the laces. And I'm sure any child psychologist would tell you that a mother's wishing she had the I-told-you-so that comes with being dead is probably not a healthy thing. For anybody.

Juggler's lament: The daily complaint you inflict upon anyone who will listen that enumerates, in tedious detail, all the balls you are dropping because no one can possibly manage to have so many in the air at once.

Jury of your peers: The panel of friends and acquaintances you carefully assemble to advise you on matters both trivial and terribly important. My jury consists of my mother, sisters, and husband, and a handful of friends who are both wise enough to give me counsel and nutty enough to understand me.

A few recent issues I have resolved with the help of my jury:

- Can you be over forty and still wear short skirts?
- How much should I care about my sons' athletic performance?
- Should we go to Montreal on vacation?
- Does the fact that I hate thinking about money mean I will one day meet financial ruin?
- Is it possible to both know you are blessed and *feel* blessed?
- Why does anyone think Tori Spelling is interesting?

Just between us:
- Your black pants haven't been to the dry cleaner in two months.
- You don't know whether the cat is up to date on his leukemia shot, and you're not exactly losing sleep over it.
- You sometimes fantasize about your entire family going away and leaving you alone for about a year.
- You occasionally refrain from asking logical follow-up questions in meetings in order to end the meeting sooner. (See *Panic room*, p. 164.)
- There are several jars in the back of your refrigerator that you haven't opened since last year.
- Your hair may look pretty clean, but a little bit of dry shampoo goes a long way.

- You really have no idea what your cholesterol level is, and does it really matter, since you can never remember whether HDL is good or bad?
- Your children don't get out of bed until half an hour before school starts.
- Which means there's a fair amount of yelling in your house in the morning.
- And, no, you don't plan your outfit or pack backpacks the night before, which would be the sensible thing.

"Just let me lie down": A request-cum-plea-cum-command that, by the nature of its constant presence and persistence, has formed a path around your brain. The path is so well worn that nearly every thought process leads to it, whether you like it or not. To wit: "I am dreading that work meeting today because I am going to see that person who really bothers me and I just don't know how to handle him ... oh, just let me lie down." Or "My daughter needs help with her math homework, but for the life of me I can't remember why a squared plus b squared equals c squared, or why anybody should care ... please, just let me lie down." This is something that your mother constantly used to say when you were a kid, and you never understood it. Why would anybody want to lie down in the middle of the day? Now that you are a mother yourself, you see that lying down in the middle of the day is the ultimate luxury, the cure for whatever might ail you, the road to redemption, the golden ticket.

Just a second: That eternity between when a child says he'll do something you've asked and when he actually gets around to it.

"Just very ambitious": The worst thing anyone can ever say about you (yes, even worse than "She's a terrible mother"). This description, which in my experience is a one-sentence opportunity killer, is simply transparent code for "a complete asshole," "lacks common sense," "doesn't understand the long view," "doesn't play well with others," and "would not hesitate to throw her own mother under a bus." In short, you never want to work with, work for, or hire someone who meets this description. And if you yourself are ever described this way — well, you've seriously got to work on your message.

Kafka was here
Kill the messenger
Kingdom of No
The kissing hand

Kafka was here: The moments at work that are so odd and make so little rational sense that the only explanation is that the ghost of Franz Kafka has made a brief guest appearance. These moments can take the form of a phone call from your child, reporting that the pet dog has eaten the pet bird (which happened to my boss), or an incompetent person who sits down in your office and demands a promotion (which has happened to me more times than I care to remember).

Kill the messenger: The action you must take in order to forget about the office for a time — that is, to remove your BlackBerry/iPhone/Treo/whatever from your person and store it as far away as your neurotic self will allow. Maybe you put it in your purse; maybe you put it in a drawer in your kitchen. But your BlackBerry/iPhone/Treo/whatever has to go somewhere else, because if you keep it within reach, it will blink or buzz nonstop, and you will not be able to resist checking your e-mail when you should instead, say, be listening to your child tell you again that he wants a drum set, and why it is crucial that you get it now rather than wait for his birthday. Despite the fact that there is always the thrill of the new with e-mail and you've heard this drum-set appeal at least nine times, you must resist. Otherwise you might as well never come home from work at all.

Any working mom worth her salt knows that it's the integrate-separate ratio between work and home that determines long-term working-motherhood success. A cautionary tale: Last year my oldest son needed to have four teeth pulled by an oral surgeon in preparation for getting braces. I accompanied him into the procedure room, which I regretted as soon as the oral surgeon began his work; specifically, watching my son's foot twitch and hearing one of his teeth crack — yes, *crack* — was more than I could handle on a Tuesday afternoon. To take my mind off the proceedings, I pulled my BlackBerry from my bag and e-mailed a colleague. On the way home my son, whose mouth was packed with gauze, muttered to me, "I can't believe you were on your *BlackBerry.*" Oh, the shame. Apparently my integrate-separate ratio had gone out of whack.

The moral of this story: when you are accompanying your child to an important, scary, and perhaps gruesome medical appointment, it is generally smarter to leave work behind, even if you think you might vomit or faint. (And if you're sure he can't see you from the padded chair, with an oral surgeon standing between the two of you — he can.) I have also found that reading work documents or talking on your cell to the office while you are waiting in the school gym for your son's choral concert to start is generally not a good idea, as it sends the message that you think there are much more important things to do than to sit in a school gym. Other places where I have been tempted to work but have thought better of it: high school orientation sessions, church, Sunday soccer games, Water Country USA.

But often integration is, if not unavoidable, at least advisable. For example, I am actually on vacation with my family as I type this sentence. My husband is skiing with my two older sons, my youngest is napping, my sister Valerie is making dry toast for my nephew, who spent the entire night throwing up, and my father is reading the paper on the sofa as he elevates the wrist that he fractured yesterday while barreling down a run that none of us should have been on in the first place (see *Image consultant,* p. 99). I just finished answering work e-mails, and I couldn't be happier.

I rarely go on vacation without doing a bit of work, for a number of reasons involving workflow, workload, and unresolved psychological issues (see *Separation anxiety,* p. 198). The first time I got a FedEx package from the office while on vacation, my friend Dan — who was sitting at the lunch table as the FedEx truck drove up — gave me a long, disappointed lecture about keeping work out of my leisure time. Dan has known me most of my life, including when I was a very silly girl who drank a lot of beer and had a bad perm, so part of him wondered: *Who is this person, taking work so seriously? Not the Kristin I know.* I had to explain to Dan that reading page proofs on vacation didn't mean I was any less silly than I had always been; it merely meant that, as a working mom, I could make it to the kindergarten Valentine's party and the pediatrician appointments and the field trip to Ellis Island with the fourth grade. Because I am always sort of working, I told Dan, I am sort of never really working. But Dan, who is a lawyer, does not believe in integrating work into home life. Which is fine for him, not only because he has a set billing structure (in which every six minutes must be accounted for), but also because he is not a working mom.

Back to my vacation. As part of her job, my sister Valerie regularly has 8:00 a.m. conference calls to discuss the sales figures from the day before; this morning's conference call was at 9:00, and she took it in her pajamas. She appears to be in touch with her office at all hours of the day and night, whether she's on vacation or not. But she also teaches Sunday school and attends her kids' thousands of sporting events and — most impressive of all — always knows where the bin of outgrown clothes is in her attic, so she can pass it on to the next sister with a younger child. In short, she is a highly functional working mom who appears to have the integrate-separate ratio just right. On this vacation Valerie skied with her BlackBerry in a little nylon pouch around her neck, hidden under her jacket. Which is either sad or brilliant, depending on how you look at it. Dan would no doubt be disappointed. As for me, I understand.

Kingdom of No: A magical land that exists only in your fantasies, where "no" is always the answer and you never feel guilty for saying it. This is the place you'd really like to be living in whenever any of the following things happens: your son's teacher asks you to take Mr. Twinkles the hamster home for the summer; a class mom asks you to bake pumpkin muffins for the Thanksgiving celebration; your babysitter asks for an extra week off, with pay; a recent graduate of your alma mater asks for an informational interview; a less recent graduate of your alma mater asks to take just a bit of your time so she can tell you how much the school would like you to contribute to the general scholarship fund; or anybody who works for you asks to see you "for ten minutes," which means they're either pregnant or quitting.

The kissing hand: The little things a working mother does to remind her children how much she loves them when they are apart.

The kissing hand is an idea that my sister Claire took from a children's book, and it goes like this: Before Claire leaves for work, she gives each of her three children a peck on the palm and tells them that if they miss her while she's gone, all they need to do is press palm to cheek and the kiss will still be there. Sometimes Claire will see her daughter give herself a little reassuring pat on the cheek when she doesn't know Mom is watching.

If your child is too old for the kissing hand (imagine try-ing it on a fourteen-year-old), there are other small ways to let her know during the day that you are thinking about her:

nonembarrassing text messages; nonembarrassing e-mails; notes in her snack bag; notes in her backpack; notes under her pillow if you are on a business trip; and the occasional call on her cell phone (but make sure to manage your expectations if she is with her friends; during those times you technically do not exist unless someone suddenly needs a ride, money, or food).

Leap of faith
Learned helplessness
Life savers
List paradox
Loosey Tooseys
Love, actually

Leap of faith: The action you take every single day of your working life when you blithely head to the office and leave your children in the care of someone else. This is truly crippling for some working mothers; when I encounter a woman who is overwhelmed with sadness and paranoia about leaving her kids with another person (babysitter, day care center staff, sometimes even husband), I both feel sorry for the woman and wonder what is wrong with me.

But we all have our coping mechanisms. Mine is "I could get hit by a bus." As in: my babysitter could be cursing like a sailor all day long; the peanut butter I'm about to eat could contain salmonella; a bomb could go off in midtown Manhattan; and I could get hit by a bus.

If you thought too much about any of those things, you'd never get out of bed in the morning. *They are all possible.* Statistically improbable on any given day, but possible. And so: the leap of faith. I will not get hit by a bus today. Midtown Manhattan will be explosion-free. This peanut butter does not contain salmonella. My babysitter does not curse in front of my child. I can keep going to work.

Learned helplessness: The epiphenomenon that micromanagers unwittingly cause in everyone around them; or yet one more example of why micromanagers have no one but themselves to blame. If you make your children's sandwiches every day, your husband will never know whether they prefer mustard or mayonnaise. If you always hang up your children's coats, they will never realize that there is a coat closet. If you don't let anyone who works for you make their own decisions, pretty soon they'll all be coming to you for permission to use the bathroom. And is that a very good use of your time?

Life savers:
- That little hand in yours
- A canceled business lunch
- Exercise before work
- Getting a hello text message from your teenager in the middle of the workday
- Slow cookers, sometimes
- A boss who does not care about face time
- A child who runs to greet you at the door
- A dog who runs to greet you at the door once the child is a teenager
- Tide to Go
- Clorox wipes

- YouTube
- A good read for your commute

List paradox: The Catch-22 of managing your life. You make a to-do list because it enables you to feel as if you are in control of your life and helps you see what you can accomplish. Therefore it boosts your self-esteem. However, there will always be more items on your list than you can actually cross off, which makes you feel worse. And so you start to cheat: writing things on your list that you have already done just so you can cross them off. And cheating is definitely bad for your self-esteem.

Loosey Gooseys: The family you admire for its relaxed attitude toward many things others find important, while you hope no one sees your family that way.

We all know some Loosey Gooseys. They are the people who are never on time for anything, whose children lose their soccer jerseys by the third game of the season, who don't sign their kids up for summer camp until May, who may not eat vegetables for four days straight and frequently forget to brush their teeth.

And they are brilliant, and a lot of fun. They live in the moment. They know soccer jerseys can be replaced and that four days without vegetables never killed anybody. Without intending to, they make you feel inferior, what with all your bourgeois concerns.

But on your darkest days, you fear that *you* are the Loosey Gooseys. And then you yell at everybody in your family about what a mess the whole house is and, to calm yourself down, have to spend three hundred dollars at the Container Store (the same amount the Loosey Gooseys are spending on a spur-of-the-moment trip to Six Flags Great Adventure).

Love, actually: The moment you realize that the feeling you have for (some of) your colleagues is not admiration or respect or affection but actually…love.

A couple of years ago one of my favorite work friends left our magazine to take another job. As we said our final good-byes, she gave me a hug and a peck on the cheek and said, "I love you." Startled, I replied, "I love you too." The moment reminded me of the scene in *Terms of Endearment* when Shirley MacLaine tells Jack Nicholson that she loves him and he tries to wriggle out of responding, finally giving her his stock answer: "I love you too, kid." The fact that I was reminded of this scene bothered me, because part of its brilliance is that Nicholson both does and does not mean it when he returns the sentiment. And the more I thought about it, the more I realized that my "I love you" had been completely sincere.

I am not a big "I love you" person. Yesterday I was listening to the radio in the car and I heard Natasha Bedingfield shout "I love you, Cubby!" to a local DJ. *What is wrong with her?* I thought to myself. Where I come from, saying "I love you" willy-nilly to every acquaintance and DJ in your life just cheapens the phrase, rendering it nearly useless on the occasions when you actually mean it. I am not sure this is healthy or even true; it's just how I was raised.

So "I love you" does not come up often at work, at least not in my experience. But the more I thought about the unexpected exchange with my beloved coworker, the more I wondered if it should. Anybody over the age of three knows there are many kinds of love: maternal love, romantic love, fraternal love, love of country, love of self, and so on. The love you have for certain coworkers is a whole other category, hard to define but lodged somewhere between maternal and fraternal, with maybe a bit of self-love thrown in. But unlike the love you have for your family and friends, love for coworkers is not something you are encouraged to express. For example, imagine what it might do to performance reviews: "Susan, you have had a very productive year. You have landed five new accounts; you are a skilled problem solver and an excellent manager. I love you." I just don't think society is ready.

One of the most embarrassing things that ever happened to me on the job was when I inadvertently called my boss "Mom." It was my first job in New York, at a small film production company; the offices were on the first floor of a brownstone, and the couple who owned the company, a commercial director and his wife, lived upstairs. The wife, Raquel, handled the finances, and she was a wonderful woman. She was a bit younger than my mother, but not by much, and there was a maternal aspect to my dealings with her; I'm sure the fact that I effectively worked in her house had something to do with that. We were both a bit surprised when I called her "Mom," and I never made the mistake again. But, looking back, clearly I loved Raquel.

Many people who rise to leadership positions do so in part because they can control their emotions (see *Emotional tourniquet,* p. 63). Sometimes I think the only reason I have been hired to run a magazine is because I'm able to remember to keep a box of tissues in my office and I can usually remain dry-eyed while others around me burst into tears. I'm sure there are individuals I work with who pity my children, raised as they are by a woman who appears to have no emotions but the occasional flash of anger. To those colleagues: I assure you, I do tell my children and my husband that I love them. At least every once in a while.

We all talk about "work/life" as if those two things were competing forces. And often they are: they compete for time, attention, brainpower, energy, space on your calendar. But when it comes to matters of the heart, it's all one big sloppy stew. If I try to think about the love I have for Jackie at my office compared to the love I have for Sharene down the street, I just get confused. Their roles in my life are completely different: I am Jackie's boss; I am Sharene's friend. I have no idea how Jackie behaves at home and no idea how Sharene behaves at work, and so you could argue that I don't completely *know* either one of them. And yet the feelings exist, even if I can't always explain them.

There have been a number of times in my current position when I've thought I was going to make a job change. It's coming, of course; the fact that I will eventually leave this job is like a train whistle in the distance—I hear it, I'm just not sure how far away it is. But one day I'm going to see the train pulling into the station, and then I will have to get on it. When I think about leaving, about reinventing myself in another organization, as so many of us do throughout our careers, there is something inherently exciting in the idea: I love change, I love a challenge, I love the new. But then I think about this cozy family of people I have become so comfortable living with. I do not love all of them; some of them actually make me feel like my hair is on fire. But when I think about leaving the ones that I do love—and yes, Jackie, that includes you—I could almost start crying and never stop.

Macromanaging

Madwoman in the attic

Magical thinking

Managing expectations

Maternity leave

Midconversation screen saver

Mission statement

Mom, interrupted

Mother load

Musical beds

Macromanaging: The talent of the truly evolved; that is, to be completely in charge without sweating the details.

Madwoman in the attic: Any deluded mother who actually thinks "working from home" is possible.

Ah, "working from home." Doesn't that have a nice ring to it? So do "owning an island" and "flat abs," and they are all equally unattainable. I have attempted working from home on many days throughout my career, and there are many attempts yet to come. But my productivity on those days resembles that of an ant traveling in and out of an anthill. Our little ant is always moving, and does seem to have a sense of purpose. But there are so many distractions! You think to yourself, *I'll just do this one quick thing and then I'll go back to work,* but one quick thing leads to another, and before you know it, you're miles away from the anthill.

For example: say I walk my son to school on a "working from home" day. Instead of proceeding directly to the train, as

I normally would, I walk back home, which leads to me pulling a weed next to the front door; which leads to a larger weeding project; which leads to a trip to the garden center; which leads to mulching; which leads to cutting flowers to put in a vase inside; which leads to iced tea in the living room, where I can admire my arrangement; which leads to looking at my watch and realizing it's time to pick my son up from school.

Magical thinking:

- If you leave the house with a stain on your shirt, people will think it happened on the way to work and there was nothing you could do about it.
- If you make it your teenager's responsibility to set his alarm and get up in the morning, he will get up without your prompting.
- If you yell at your son to try to get him out the door faster in the morning, that should do the trick.
- If you give the elementary school your work phone as your daytime number, the school will not leave messages on your home phone.
- If you spend your day apart from your kids, they will tell you every little detail about their day during dinner.
- If a child comes into your room in the middle of the night and wakes you up, you will not start thinking about work.
- If you tell your husband that you have a work event next Tuesday night, he will definitely remember.

- If you take a day off, you will hide your BlackBerry in a drawer and will not look at your e-mail once.

Managing expectations: The behavior modification you must adopt when dealing with pregnant colleagues. In short, expect very little. She may appear to be engaged in the workplace issue at hand, but what she's really thinking is, *Good Lord, that was quite a kick! Is it possible that this baby could damage one of my organs? Has that ever happened? Note to self: go online as soon as this meeting is over, which had better be soon, because I really have to pee.*

Maternity leave: The five minutes at the beginning of any meeting that you must spend talking about labor and delivery if there is a pregnant colleague in the room. If the pregnant colleague is more than thirty-seven weeks along or there are only women present, this section of the meeting may stretch to as long as fifteen minutes. Topics to cover: the need for an epidural, doulas, midwives, inducing labor, sciatica, men who don't get it.

Midconversation screen saver: The thing that unexpectedly happens when your husband is talking and suddenly you start thinking about whether you should take that chicken out of the freezer to defrost and if you should wear your black pants to work tomorrow because it's only Monday and you might be able to get away with wearing them twice in one week without anyone noticing if you put enough days in between. Your husband thinks you are still listening, but you have gone on screen saver. Sometimes you go on screen saver involuntarily; sometimes—particularly if your husband is talking about how Somebody United just beat FC Whosie-whatsit—you can force it to happen.

Mission statement: The explanation you are forced to provide to children or coworkers whenever you want the group to do something that is meeting intense resistance. Examples include family trips to museums, budget cutting.

Mom, interrupted: In a nutshell, your existence. From the moment children enter your life, you will never again have a lengthy adult conversation, finish a home improvement project, or complete a work assignment to your satisfaction before it's time to rush out of the office to relieve the babysitter.

Mother load: The hard, enduring truth that you are selfish and your mother is not, and that you must pay her selflessness forward to your own children, who may never thank you and certainly will never love you as much as you love them.

Motherhood is not a relationship of emotional equals. At a certain point—in my experience, around age nine—your children cease to be as interested in you as you are in them. They do not think of you constantly during the day, as you do them. Some children are more polite than others and, even as teenagers, will continue to ask you about work, or hug you when you look like you are going to cry, or bring you breakfast in bed on your birthday. But for the most part they become much more concerned with what their friends think of them and whether or not they will feel like giant losers forever, or just until they turn twenty-one. I guess this is how it should be. They should not always need your guidance, or even necessarily your opinion. Still, there is something heartbreaking in watching your child take a deep breath, square his shoulders, and sail away in his own little boat, without so much as a backward glance. The waters may be calm or filled with whitecaps, and there's not much you can do about it either way. You can merely observe, and hope for the best.

When I was a child I thought my mother was perfect, in part because of the many wonderful things she did for me. There was the implicit understanding that everything I did and felt and wanted was more important than anything she might do, feel, or want. Now that I am an adult, the unequal nature of our relationship pains me, although when I was a child everything seemed just right. My mother was always there for me, and she always had the answer I needed. She was fair, compassionate, curious, energetic. She had (and still has) a no-nonsense approach to nearly everything, and did not believe in a problem without a solution. She was a bit of a worrier, but she knew when worry was taking an unproductive turn; then she would say, "Drop that rock." She is up to any challenge, which she calls the " 'Oh, I can do that' disease." Apparently it plagues all the women in our family.

My mother taught me that the happiest individuals in the world are those who put other people first, which is exactly what she has done—and continues to do—as a mother. Over time I have come to see that she does not have all the answers. For example, she is not a lot of help when an acquaintance dies and you do not know whether to go to the viewing, the funeral, or both. She is inherently suspicious of babysitters, although she seems to be softening a bit as her grandchildren get older and are proving to be more or less normal. She still firmly believes that all females over the age of ten must wear a slip with a skirt. She does not know how to get wax off a sterling silver candlestick and she has an unfortunate tendency to overcook vegetables. Other than that, she is good at almost everything.

When I was in college my parents would call me every Sunday night. This was back in the day when cell phones didn't exist and a long-distance conversation seemed as extravagant as a trip to Tahiti. I would give them the minute details of my week, incredibly boring stuff in retrospect, and they seemed interested in all of it. After college the weekly calls continued, supplemented by bursts of constant contact when I was either in labor with a grandchild or had an urgent need (such as when I hosted my first Easter dinner; I will never forget my mother remarking to my father, "She's twenty-seven years old and doesn't know how to bake a ham!"). Now that I am much more pressed for time, and have so many main characters in my little life dramedy, it is often the case that my mother is more interested in the details of my week than I am. But it's all part of the same message: she is the giver; I am the taker. She is still the marsupial mother carrying me around in her pouch, and I'm still enjoying the ride.

I am replicating that relationship with my own boys; I suppose this is what they mean by "pay it forward." Although, honestly, being unselfish is so hard that I wonder if it's completely necessary. Say I am eating a bowl of ice cream and one of my sons asks for the last bite. Is it OK for me to say no? Similarly, if one of my boys wants me to lie down with him before he falls asleep and all I want to do is get into my own bed and have a few minutes to myself, can I refuse? Denying requests like these does not seem right. But what about "If Mama ain't happy, ain't nobody happy"? Because there are definitely days when Mama wants that last spoonful of ice cream, and she doesn't want to lie down with you either.

Unless you are a complete narcissist, you raise children with the expectation that after a certain age, they will not think about you all that much. At least not until they begin to worry about your health, and then you become a depressing topic of conversation, as in "What are we going to do about Mom?" But there is a long period in between their early childhood and your eventual demise when they are focusing on their own lives and you need to find something else to do. Enter work. When your children are young, you work to keep alive that part of you that does not wholly enjoy, say, throwing pebbles into a puddle with a toddler thirty-seven times in a row. When your children are older, work is a different sort of refuge: you are needed there. If you don't show up at work, your coworkers worry. If you don't show up at home, your teenage children have a party and eventually your neighbors call the police. But you will forgive your children, just as you forgive them for being the takers while you remain the giver. That is the mother load, whether your children ever realize it or not.

Musical beds: The nightly game you play, unless you are one of those unusual families with no sleeping problems. (If so, it's people like you who give pediatricians the false impression that if you just apply a firm hand in the bedtime routine, all will be fine.)

On any given night in our house, here's what you might find:

- Kids on our floor
- Kids on their own floor, with two twin mattresses shoved together
- One parent on the kids' floor (rare, but it's happened)
- One kid on the bench at the foot of our bed
- One kid on the bench at the foot of our bed, another on a foam mattress on our floor
- Kids together in a single bed in their room
- Kids in our bed
- Kids together in the queen-size bed in the guest room

And then there's the matter of the pets. (See *Very, verrrryyyyy sleeeeeeepy...*, p. 224.)

Nanny envy

Negative feedback loop

No child left behind

"Not on the menu"

"No visibility on that right now"

Nanny envy: The inevitable emotion you feel when you encounter a babysitter who possesses even one positive quality that yours doesn't. Nanny envy can strike at any time. The only cure? Money. Spend the absolute maximum you can for child care, in the hope that you really do get what you pay for. Then you will find a gem who inspires nanny envy in other mothers, who will be so nice to her that you will become convinced they are trying to steal her away.

Negative feedback loop: Your house is messy and the kids won't brush their teeth and the dinner dishes are still in the sink and everything around you is just cluttered and bad and why did you marry that man in the first place and how did you get yourself into all this and why doesn't anyone but you see that the dog is at the back door and needs to be let in and if someone would just go through the mail more than once a week you would not have that giant pile on the counter, filled no doubt with at least three bills that are overdue.

Of course, you really just need to break the loop somehow. Try going to bed. Immediately.

No child left behind: The reminder running through the head of nearly every working mother after just one brush with disaster.

All mothers have a story: My friend Janice left her newborn in his car seat in the front hall while the rest of the family took off for Boston. (Luckily, they made it only down the block.) My neighbor Ann locked her toddler in the car and had to explain to a two-year-old how to work the automatic lock. And then there was the time I left my son at church.

It was the day of our third child's christening; both sets of grandparents were in town and we were hosting a lunch celebration after the service. I was a little tense, managing the details of the party and trying, as the mother of a three-month-old, to plan my every move around the need to breast-feed on a moment's notice. Then my sister showed up at the church and announced that she had driven off with her wallet on the roof of her car from a gas station on the Long Island Expressway, leaving her credit cards and all manner of identification — identification that she was going to need the following day, when she had to get on the company plane with her CEO — in some ditch who knows where. So then I was tense about the party, the potential need to breast-feed in the middle of the christening, and whether or not my sister was going to have her identity stolen before we sat down for lunch.

As divine luck would have it, the service was wonderful. My baby wore a beautiful christening gown with lace at the neck that had belonged to some great-great-somebody-or-other on my husband's side of the family, and although he did a big poo before it was time for him to go up to the altar, nobody knew it but me. After the ceremony we all piled back into various cars to rush home in time for the arrival of the food, which turned out to be late. I was spinning further into the nervous vortex when the phone rang. Surely it was the restaurant. "Hello?!" I shouted into the phone. There was a little voice on the other end. "It's OK, Mom," my eight-year-old middle child said. "I can just get a ride home with Terry and Elizabeth."

The most alarming thing about leaving him at the church—at least it was a *church,* and not a pool hall—is that I didn't actually assume he was in a car with another family member, although I certainly could have lied and said I did. I just *forgot him*. And to think that I actually considered *Home Alone* a silly movie. How many therapy sessions do you think my son will get out of *that* little episode?

"Not on the menu": The best way to explain the absence of a personality trait or skill that you wished you possessed but never will. I learned this from my work friend Grant. Several years ago we were discussing a mutual acquaintance who lacks a certain empathy when it comes to dealing with others. "Well," Grant said with a shrug, "you know with her that's just not on the menu."

A few things that are not on my menu:

- Staying up past midnight
- Talking on the phone for fun
- Creating an Excel spreadsheet
- Making crepes
- Being diplomatic
- Understanding macroeconomics
- Facing dental appointments without fear
- Sucking up to people at work who just seem idiotic
- Setting career goals
- Whistling
- Committing unconditionally to exercise

I can live without understanding macroeconomics and making crepes. I can also live with my fear of the dentist, because I hear they make pills for just such a problem. I will never be able to suck up to idiotic people at work, which may or may not ultimately be my downfall, just as my inability to stay up past midnight may one day cause my husband to leave me for a woman who will watch *David Letterman* with him. However, I do worry about my lack of commitment to exercise. If I don't start to work out thirty minutes a day, as all the women's magazines tell me to, I will significantly shorten my life span, and so I will never learn to whistle. And I've been trying really hard to whistle since I was about five, and would very much like to master it before they put me in the grave.

Let's start with the exercise recommendations. Who has

time to exercise thirty minutes a day? I suppose I do, but then I don't have time to hold down a job or be a good mother, and when push comes to shove, those two requirements always win out. Then there's the exercise versus sleep tug-of-war (see *Zero-sum living,* p. 255), and you're never really sure how that's going to turn out on any given morning. The sad thing is, I really enjoy exercise, both the activity and the result. I have always been fairly athletic, except for four years in college when I was too busy drinking beer and eating Mint Milano cookies to go running. I like the treadmill (even if it confronts me with unpleasant metaphors for my working and home lives) and I like the elliptical machine because it's easy on my knees. I like to lift weights, once I can get past the preening, sleeveless men grunting at themselves in the gym mirror. I even like the ergometer, except for the fact that I can never let go of the "oars" to wipe my sweaty face. Can't somebody do something about that? I love to run outside, rain or shine. But exercising during the week requires me to wake up at 5:30, and some days I just can't do it. Especially in the winter, when it's still dark at 5:30, because, as everybody knows, getting up in the dark is depressing and unnatural and will eventually turn you into a full-blown lunatic.

And so there is the constant disappointment with my body, specifically with the area between my rib cage and knees. It is a universally held truth that as a woman gets older, her pants get tighter, even if her weight does not change. Based on personal experience, this phenomenon begins when you are forty. There's really very little you can do about it except perhaps do a headstand for the thirty minutes you should be exercising every day, as a way to combat the forces of gravity. And no, you cannot blame your children for the tight-pants problem, just as you cannot say that the reason you are overweight is because you were once pregnant and "never lost the baby weight." You can, however, blame your children for the fact that you don't have time to exercise, because this is probably the truth. If you are me, part of the reason you don't have time to exercise is because you spend all your free time watching *them* exercise, as you sit on the sidelines just feeling your thighs getting fatter.

Of course, it's not really the fault of your children. At the end of the day, your job is to blame. It's simply not possible to spend most of your time sitting in meetings and expect that your rear end is going to be improved by the experience. I have found that when I am in a meeting it's best not to look down, especially if the meeting is a boring one, because the sight of my decidedly unflat stomach sends me to a dark place and makes the people around me suddenly seem intolerable. Helpful magazine articles advise you to "exercise at your desk," which as far as I'm concerned is an absolutely ridiculous notion. I cannot imagine doing leg lifts in front of my computer. For starters, my pants are too tight.

Of course, any decent chef is always tweaking his menu. Although it might not appear at the moment, a serious commitment to exercise will be right at the top of my menu someday — perhaps when I'm not spending so much of my life at kids' soccer games. Then I expect to have all the time in the world to do headstands and leg lifts wherever I please. Let's just hope I live that long.

"No visibility on that right now": The most glorious corporate-bullshit-speak I have ever heard from a person of importance who didn't want to say "I don't know." It was during the Q and A portion of a management presentation; when I heard it I thought, *I've got to try that at home.* However, in response to questions such as "Do we have any ice cream?" and "Do I really have to go to church tomorrow?" it just confuses the audience.

OCEAN
One angry mother
Operation shock and awe
Oppositional advantage, or
    Newton's law meets your life

OCEAN: The acronym that those who study personality use to understand people; also known as the Big Five: openness, conscientiousness, extroversion, agreeability, neuroticism. I have found that these five are quite helpful in evaluating not just all of your friends and relatives, but any babysitter you consider hiring. To wit, a few situations I've encountered over the years:

Openness: Will she be honest about the real reason she had to take an extra week off to go to the Dominican Republic, or when she returns and you politely inquire about her alleged boyfriend's sister's wedding, does she look at you blankly and reply, "What wedding?"

Conscientiousness: Will she call your office to tell you that your screen door has partially blown off its hinges and is resting at a weird angle against the house, or will she just let you be surprised when you arrive home from work?

Extroversion: Can she have a productive conversation with the following people: school secretary; plumber; guy behind the counter at the post office; man delivering furniture that may or may not be damaged; all other babysitters, no matter where they're from; snooty moms who treat her like a second-class citizen?

Agreeability: If the receptionist at the pediatric dentist's office is a bit rude to her, will she get into an argument that results in the receptionist writing you a note requesting that from now on *you* take your son to get his cavities filled?

Neuroticism: Is she so afraid of snakes and lizards that she will run out of the room if your son is wearing a Pablo Python T-shirt—that's right, just a picture of a reptile printed on a T-shirt—from camp at the Bronx Zoo?

One angry mother: Any woman who is over the age of forty and trying to balance a job, a husband, children, and running a household. If she has any pets, then she may be extra angry. Maybe it's hormones; maybe it's life stage; maybe it's mortality nipping at the heels, but most of the over-forty working moms I know are *just pissed off.* Still, they sure do get a lot done.

Operation shock and awe: When you are able to show your children—if only for a fleeting moment—that you are not merely the humorless taskmaster with the frown lines on the bridge of her nose, but someone who is actually cool and interesting. Sort of. Operations can include but are not limited to: doing a front flip off a diving board; whistling with a blade of grass between your thumbs; knowing all the words to "Don't Stop Believin'," or to any other song on Guitar Hero for that matter; meeting someone really famous; flying first-class on a work trip; getting pregnant and keeping it a secret, at least for the first trimester.

Oppositional advantage, or Newton's law meets your life: The fact that having two opposing forces in your life — work and children — vastly improves your ability to put things into perspective. The greatest advantage this presents is that when people or situations go awry in the workplace, as a working mother you are able to say, "Oh, honestly, does it really matter? At least no one is bleeding."

The only way I am certain that Sir Isaac Newton knew what he was talking about is not because I paid that much attention in high school physics, but because I continued to work after having children, thus proving in my own small way that to every action (pursuing a career) there is an equal and opposite reaction (trying to raise children). If you take a look at my daily life, it would appear that the kids and the job are on equal footing: both require enormous amounts of my time and make me feel proud of my accomplishments while I wonder how I've managed to con people around me into believing I know what I'm doing. There is nothing equal about the *importance* of children versus work in my life, despite what the hours tell you, but they are forces in opposition. And the tension between them provides a benefit to each: there are a handful of ways in which working makes me a better parent (for one, I can't micromanage my kids' every move, which appears to benefit all of us) and countless ways in which being a mother makes me better at work. Starting with the fact that the existence of my children allows me to put so much of the work nonsense into perspective, and not go completely out of my mind from Monday to Friday, week after week.

First, consider the magnitude of the problems at work versus those at home. Truly job-threatening situations aside, most work problems pale in comparison to those in the domestic sphere. When I am at work, I never have to monitor someone's temperature in case he has an ear infection and is going to be up half the night, for example. In my work life, I've never had to rush anyone to the emergency room to get thirty-two stitches. At the office, I've never faced disappointment and confusion quite like the time the tooth fairy failed to appear, despite the giant molar carefully stowed under my son's pillow. (This happened last week, and I don't think either of us has gotten over it.) There is occasional crying at work, but nothing compared to the crying at home. Ditto whining. At work I don't have to answer questions about why life is so unfair, why brothers are so awful, why there are cemeteries, what masturbation is, and what we're doing about the fact that human beings are ruining the earth. When coworkers are searching their souls or having existential crises, they do so in the privacy of their own heads and need no help from me. At home there appears to be an existential crisis once a day, and somehow I am always implicated.

And the times of achievement! Like most of us, I have known work triumphs that put a spring in my step for days, weeks, months. Still, nothing can compare with moments like the one we had at home last night, when our toddler finally pooped on his little toddler-sized potty. Although he greeted this event with bewilderment and cautious optimism, the over-the-top nature of his mother's reaction convinced him that this was indeed a very happy occasion. When was the last time there was an accomplishment of such magnitude at the office? I honestly can't remember. But when I survey the events of just the past week at home, I can point to a number of important, celebration-worthy achievements: my eighth grader got straight As on his report card; my fifth grader had three RBIs at his baseball game; and the little guy pooped on the potty. Exciting week!

I often fantasize about the lives of my colleagues who do not have children. I imagine coming home at the end of the day and sitting down with a glass of wine to have a sustained conversation with my husband, or even with Brian Williams on the nightly news. I dream about reading a page-turner in bed with no one else around (including sons who like nothing better than to see if they can vault onto the mattress without their feet ever touching the bench that sits at the foot of the bed—in my experience, a sure concentration-breaker). I fantasize about sleeping until 7:30 during the week and having no one to get out the door but myself, which some mornings feels complicated enough.

I would never suggest that working women with children are wiser than those without; I know plenty of geniuses and idiots in both groups. But I wonder: if I did not have the opposition of family, would I ever be able to put work behind me at the end of the day? When I leave the office I close a door, both literally and metaphorically, and open another one when I come home. If I did not have my children, would I find another door to open, or would my brain be trapped in the office all night long? I fear I would become one of those people at work who "cares too much," which is code for "too intense/serious/boring/can't relate well to others/totally uncool/will eventually have to go." Being a mother makes me better at my job, because it makes me care without really caring. And that's the only thing that seems to work for me.

Palate cleanser
Panic room
Paper chase
Perfomance anxiety
Pie chart of you
Planning your own demise
Pregnant pause
Primary school monomania
PTSD

Palate cleanser: The activity that helps you transition from your work life to your home life and vice versa. It may be listening to NPR in the car; knitting on the bus; gossiping with friends on the train. I have two categories of palate cleanser, one for the train ride to work and one for the train ride home. On my way to work I either read the paper or answer e-mails on my BlackBerry. Occasionally I will read my book-group book, particularly if it is available in paperback (not too heavy to lug), although reading a novel on the way to work feels like having dessert before eating dinner.

On the way home from work I read another paper (this one a tabloid), *People* or *Vogue* or *House Beautiful* or *Vanity Fair,* or my book-group novel, or I talk to my husband. If I absolutely must, I answer work e-mails, but that just serves to obliterate the entire palate cleansing effect and leave a very bad taste in my mouth for the rest of the day.

Panic room: Any place where you are held hostage by a meeting that is going on longer than necessary and is conducted by people who apparently have nothing else to do for the rest of the day. And so you grow increasingly anxious, especially when you start thinking about the eighty-five unanswered e-mails back at your desk or the fact that you haven't planned anything for dinner. Although you may feel hostility toward the ridiculous time-wasters around you who couldn't spell the word *efficiency* if you held a gun to their heads, your overriding sense is one of panic: "Oh. My. God! Are we all going to have to spend the night here?!?!?!?!?!?"

Paper chase: The nerve-racking hunt for the Very Important Elementary School Form at 9:30 p.m. on the night before it is due, as it has suddenly disappeared from the spot by the phone where it has been getting in the way for the last week and a half and is now crumpled up in some nether region of your kitchen. (Note: The number of Very Important Elementary School Forms you must fill out does not directly correspond to the number of children you have; if you have one child, you have x number of forms, but if you have three children, the number grows not to x times three but to x times seven. This equation changes dramatically when one of your children reaches middle school, at which point nearly all forms for that child cease and your search for information takes a very different shape: calling other parents, trying to make sense of the school website, occasional spying.)

Performance anxiety: The fear that you will show up at work one morning and realize that your mental hard drive has been completely erased overnight. The years of trying to remember important dates on the school calendar as well as the names of all the supporting characters in your daily work life — not to mention the gazillion passwords you have for the gazillion things in your life that can be accessed only online — will have finally taken their toll. You will be blubbering, speechless, spent, and will have to be carried out on a gurney.

Pie chart of you: The division of your personal and professional lives into sectors that, no matter how you slice them, need to add up to twenty-four hours in a day when, if life were really fair, each day would contain forty-eight hours. And so: sacrifices.

When you are very young you have all the time in the world, which is unfortunate because everything moves so slowly and you are just so bored. Everyone around you is an idiot, which makes the long days even longer. All the adults you know complain about not having enough time to get anything done, and you know that if they were just a bit more creative in their thinking or, at the very least, understood how to program the VCR, they would find they had a lot more time than they thought. And when, dear God, is life ever going to start?

Then you hit age twenty-five and you realize that you do not actually have all the time in the world. You begin to understand that time is no longer infinitely elastic, and if you are spending hours doing one thing, you are just stealing from something else. And why did no one warn you that at least 30 percent of your time would be relegated to activities that are really tedious or difficult, like trying to find a rental apartment you can afford and a nice boy you can marry and stay married to until you die? This is a terrible time of life, the midtwenties, because you still don't really know what your adulthood looks like, but you have begun to realize that time is not infinite. And you may not have children yet, which means you have a lot of time to ask yourself questions like "Who am I?" which rarely leads you down a pretty path. Luckily, as soon as you have children, you have very little time to think about existential matters, which provides a strange kind of relief.

Now, coming to terms with the fact that your time is limited — both in the macro and the micro sense — is not the same as coming to terms with how you actually spend the time you have. My friend Silvia used to be a career counselor, and a few years back she taught our book group a little exercise, which was to draw our lives as pie charts. We were sitting at dinner and after the exercise we all blithely helped ourselves to more wine, and the conversation turned to genuinely important topics, like who among the women we know had gotten breast implants. I, however, was unable to think about breasts because my pie chart was so disturbing. Why? Basically my life consisted of three segments: kids, work, and sleep.

Let's leave the husband out of it for a minute. And showering, and watching silly people do dumb things on YouTube, each of which takes up a little bit of my time on any given day. Where is gardening, which is one of my favorite activities in the world? And reading, also one of the biggies? And what about friends?!?

I may not spend enough time with my husband (no, we do not have "date nights," as couples with great marriages are apparently supposed to have), but at least I see him every day, and in the giant portion of my pie chart that is sleep he's right next to me. I can live with limiting my reading to bedtime, because falling asleep with the help of a book (which I do nearly every night, after about ten minutes' effort) seems better than falling asleep with the help of Ambien. Even gardening is something I can neglect; as much as it pains me to see ivy overtaking the columbine I planted last year, or to watch the skimmia in the front bed turn ever yellower because I mistakenly planted it in full sun, I know I can overlook my garden and then go back to it. The only price I pay is the price of having to start again.

Friends, however, are a different story. Unlike with my garden, I can't decide I'm going to forget about friends for the next fifteen years and then get a redemptive do-over once my youngest is off to college. Friendships require consistent attention and maintenance and even the occasional aggressive pruning. And currently I find it difficult to make time for that attention-maintenance-pruning in my pie chart. After kids, work, and sleep, there is just so little energy left.

Because my days are so full of people I have to see, the list of extracurricular people I want to see is extremely short. This can't be healthy. Nor, I suspect, is it healthy—or even remotely normal—to feel put out when the telephone dares to ring. I can't tell you how often we hear the phone and before it even rings twice I am shouting to my kids, "Let the machine get it!" Terrible, terrible, terrible. I receive e-mails with the subject line "Girls' Night Out!!!" and not only do I not think, *Woo-hoo!!!* as I'm undoubtedly meant to, but I just want to crawl under my desk. In short, I spend a lot of time wishing everybody would just leave me alone. Literally. Remember how Princess Diana used to go to a clinic for colonic irrigation? I think I need to go to a cabin in the middle of the woods for a humanity irrigation. That may be just the cleansing I need.

The thing is, I love people, at least as a concept. I have inherited my father's tendency to engage in conversation with any stranger who crosses my path, because you never know what you might learn from the cute waiter or the checkout girl at CVS. (This habit, as you might imagine, is a source of constant mortification for my teenage son, who doesn't understand why I can't just silently pay for the pizza or the shampoo and get back in the car.) I would not be able to get through life without friendship; my friends provide guidance, comfort, and a welcome, entertaining commercial break from the hackneyed sitcom that is sometimes my daily life. But my drive to be alone gets in the way of maintaining those relationships. And so I worry about a barren, friendless future.

My parents have a million friends. They have golf friends and skiing friends and work friends, bridge friends and tennis friends, country club and movie club and gourmet group friends. Friends they've known since college and law school and many others they've picked up along the way. Their friendship universe is a giant Venn diagram with very small areas of overlap. They are always busy doing something with friends, and when the action in one segment of the diagram seems temporarily slow, they'll move into another segment. It has always been this way; when I was a kid it seemed as if their life was one long dinner party, with brief interruptions for child care and work. They have made wise investments in friendships over time and are reaping handsome dividends.

If I refuse to participate in girls' nights out now, who will go to lunch with me when I'm seventy? When work is over and the kids are grown and sleep becomes less of a luxury, am I going to appear on the social scene to find that everyone around me is laughing at the punch line, and I'm the only one who didn't hear the setup? Will I be the one sending out woo-hoo e-mails and hoping for the best?

So that's the tension: I want to make more time for friends, but I want to be left alone, and the pie chart does not expand. Working less is currently not a viable option, and I'm not going to get rid of any of my kids, as much as I'm sometimes tempted. Which leaves sleep. I suppose, if I want to avoid that barren, friendless future, I will just have to carve some time out of the sleep portion of the pie and get out more. But with even less sleep than I'm already getting, I will be so peevish and unbearable that no one will want to be around me anyway. Which, sad to say, I may enjoy.

Planning your own demise: The unfortunate process of trying to map out every step of your life, without allowing for the influence of serendipity and fate. (See *The X Factor,* p. 241.)

Pregnant pause: The period that begins at thirty-four weeks gestation and lasts until your baby is born, during which time you find it nearly impossible to care about anything that happens at work. This phenomenon may be due to hormones, or it may be that you are distracted by the fact that your watchband is now on the last hole and it's still too tight, meaning that you are surely cutting off circulation to your left hand and it will eventually have to be amputated. And won't you need that hand to change diapers? (See *Managing expectations,* p. 137.)

Primary school monomania: The phenomenon in which school administrators and parents who don't work outside the home forget that parents like you are generally not available for PTA brainstorms, lunchtime programs, or wrapping paper sale meetings during the middle of the day. And that it's fine for the back-to-school picnic to start at 5:00 p.m., because really, isn't everyone home from work by 5:00?

PTSD: Post-Thanksgiving stress disorder. The state of extreme anxiety you experience during the month of December, what with the teacher gifts and Christmas cards and Secret Santas at work; the tipping of the garbageman and the women who make your hair look acceptable; the fact that you never know what to get your husband for Christmas, not to mention your father, who seems to have never needed anything in his whole adult life; the school Christmas concert and your own bone-headed insistence on seeing *The Nutcracker,* although you suspect you're the only one who really enjoys it; the hostess gifts and babysitter gifts and the volunteering at the soup kitchen, which you should probably do during the rest of the year instead. If it wouldn't result in your kids completely freaking out or the loss of your job, you would follow your instincts and take to your bed on Black Friday and not get up until January 2.

"Quality time"
Qué será, seráism
Questions without answers
Quest through the chaos,
    a.k.a. quest that leads straight to madness
Quitters never win

"Quality time": The hilarious, misguided notion that you can actually make your family love and value an educational group activity if you try hard enough. In my house, this is how "quality time" progresses, in five stages:

Stage 1: One parent says, "Let's do something fun with the kids. I know, how about the zoo?"

Stage 2: Genuine excitement on the part of both parents. "Kids, we're going to the zoo!" they practically shriek. All the children groan, even the baby.

Stage 3 (longest stage): A good hour of sniping and tension as the parents try to pack everybody up for the activity that the kids are dreading more and more by the minute, and they're not shy about letting parents know it.

Stage 4: Very brief stage in which the kids cling to the side of the sofa by their fingernails because all they really want to do is watch *SpongeBob SquarePants* all day. One parent's question, "Why do we bother to have a zoo membership if all you want to do is watch TV?" proves to be fairly ineffective.

Stage 5: The family heads off and undertakes the activity, which miraculously turns out to be really fun for all and leads to a satisfying I-told-you-so on the part of the parents, which the kids blithely ignore.

Qué será, seráism: Vital coping mechanism necessary for the health and survival of any working mother. Also known as letting things go; moving on; putting things in perspective; having your priorities straight; trusting fate; knowing things happen for a reason; not sweating the small stuff; not trying too hard. (See *Ignore the tray,* p. 99.)

Questions without answers:
- Why aren't husbands more helpful?
- Why do kids just want to stare at a screen all day?
- Why do working moms and stay-at-home moms make such assumptions about each other?
- Why are girls more communicative than boys?
- Why does anyone schedule a work meeting for 8:00 a.m.?
- Why don't we all have a four-day workweek?
- Why do you think about work when you wake up in the middle of the night?
- Why do so many boys want to be professional athletes when they grow up?
- Why do some people seem not to hear when you say "I've got to hang up?"

Quest through the chaos, a.k.a. quest that leads straight to madness: The search through your entire house for an important document, photo, or piece of memorabilia that your child needs to take to school—tomorrow. This quest is embarked upon in response to a seemingly innocent assignment from a teacher or fellow parent and feels so unreasonable given the amount of free time you have that you question your entire identity and wonder whether this whole "balance" thing is just a giant myth propagated by school principals, class parents, and people who need only five hours of sleep.

For instance, recently my middle son brought a note home from the yearbook committee requesting that all parents of fifth-grade students send in the school photos of their children from each grade, kindergarten through fifth, along with any candid shots they had gathered over the years. *OK,* I thought, *just kill me now.* I might as well have been asked to fly to Egypt and dig up a pharaoh. I could not begin to imagine where all of those photos were, because I am not the kind of mother who has her children's class pictures sorted by year or grade or—let's be frank—by any system whatsoever. As one who is Not That Kind of Mother, I did the only sensible thing, which was to ignore this request, hoping that either the assignment would go away, my husband would take care of it, or the photos would magically appear one morning on the kitchen counter. No such luck.

Then, predictably, the cheery reminders started appearing in my e-mail in-box, with pep-talk-type messages about how great the yearbook was going to be, if slacker parents like me who flagrantly ignore deadlines would just get off their duffs and send in the pictures. Honestly! And so I went to the immature, martyrdom place: *I have a full-time job! And three kids! And a cat who needs two medications! And a husband who doesn't get up until 7:30! And isn't it getting awfully close to Christmas?* (See *PTSD,* p. 170.) I would pass other fifth-grade parents on the walk to school, and they all looked so calm. Why weren't any of them freaking out?

You would think that by the time I had my third child, I'd get used to producing elusive information on demand. It starts the moment they begin hectoring you in the hospital to actually give your child a name, and it never stops. From old men's shirts to be made into smocks to empty coffee cans for the weather experiment to napkins for the Spanish class holiday party, it seems that every week I must produce something to send to school, and it's always due the next day. And the kids really are of limited use when it comes to searching for anything, which is reason number 7 on the list of why being a parent is so hard.

One of the worst things about a quest through the chaos is that you discover that many other parents are just as disorganized as you are, but they have the ability to put things in perspective and not go to the martyrdom place. (See *Loosey Gooseys,* p. 127.) They realize in their annoying maturity and wisdom that these things always come together in the end; you are a capable human being and therefore will find the photographs (and the man's shirt, and the empty coffee can, and the napkins). Other, calmer parents are at peace with their lack of organization, which you are not and never will be. Which is why you can never be in charge of any school committees, and why a simple chore like looking for school photos for the yearbook can make you think that homeschooling might be a decent option after all.

Quitters never win: The one thing you learned in kindergarten that is absolutely false. At a certain point quitters really do win, when quitting means eliminating a bad job from your life. Let's be honest. How many of you have dreamt of writing an out-of-office e-mail that said the following: "Having realized, after years of thankless toil, that this job/this industry/my coworkers/my measly paycheck/my crazy boss is no longer worth my valuable time, I will be out of the office for the rest of my life. If you need immediate assistance, find someone else." If that's not a win, I don't know what is.

Range of motion
Ravages of time
Recipes for disaster
Reverse-body dysmorphia
R O I
Role model reversal
Routine exam

Range of motion: The degree to which your body is able to stretch, or bend to the side, or some such. Alternatively: the degree to which you can ably manage a wide range of tasks.

I hadn't given much thought to my range of motion until I tried yoga and learned that mine is, in fact, quite limited. Come to think of it, I haven't touched my toes since 1985. But how is this possible? My range of motion in every other area of life is so big, it's unbelievable! I was tempted to ask the yoga instructor if *she* could manage a kitchen renovation and a new baby while working fifty-five hours a week—how's that for range of motion, sister?—but worried that such an impertinent question would lead to some sort of injury in class. So I kept my mouth shut, and quit yoga instead.

Ravages of time: The damage you inflict upon those around you when you find yourself with too much to do and not enough time to get it all done. It's no accident that I rarely yell at my kids or snap at my husband unless I am late or over-whelmed by a to-do list that seems to have no end.

Recipes for disaster: Things you believe you can accomplish in the kitchen during those deluded moments when you think devoting an entire day to cooking actually works with your schedule and lifestyle. Including, but not limited to, osso buco, cassoulet, and pavlova.

Reverse-body dysmorphia: When you think you—and partic-ularly the back of your thighs—look better than you really do because there was once a time when you didn't spend all day sitting on your rear end, and you still think you're living in that time. But your thighs know better. And so you go someplace in a bathing suit and expect that you will look the way you did when you were twenty-nine, until you catch a glimpse of your-self in the mirror and think, *Mom, is that you?*

ROI: The return on investment for every action you take as a working mother. For example, say you have to choose between flying to California for a meeting and attending the meeting by conference call from your office. By not being in California, you will miss personal contact, the nuances of facial expres-sions, meeting an old college friend for dinner that night. But you will gain the opportunity to attend your child's play, plus you won't have to fly, plus you will be present for six other meetings happening back at the office. When you weigh the two options, it's clear that attending the California meeting by conference call has the greater ROI.

The ROI analysis also works to guide decisions regarding family vacations, clothing purchases, what to make for dinner.

Role model reversal: When, after working for women you thought (in your naïveté and lack of experience) were "bad" mothers, you turn into exactly the sort of mother you said you would never be.

I have worked for some tough broads in my day. Women who are respected and feared in the magazine industry; women who don't suffer fools lightly, who brook no opposition, who don't take no for an answer. Women who are at the top of their game, who eat people like you for breakfast. Women who belittle others in public, just for sport; women who yell at you or look through you; women who have mastered the wordless, humiliating dismissal. It has not always been fun working for tough broads, but I've learned more than a few useful lessons. Including, I thought, precisely how not to be a mother.

For a number of years in my twenties and early thirties I worked for a woman who is universally regarded as terrifying, both by those who have worked for her and those who haven't. One day I was in her office when she was on the phone with her teenage daughter. The daughter apparently didn't like what Mom had to say, because she hung up on her. The teenage daughter, hanging up on the Most Terrifying Person in the

World! It was a thrilling moment for me, on so many levels. Not to mention a significant signal that my terrifying boss was a Bad Mother; if she didn't work so hard and was not generally such a difficult person, she would have a better relationship with her daughter, who would never, ever hang up on her.

And then I had a teenager. And one day I picked up the phone to talk to him while I was in the middle of a meeting in my office, and told him something he did not want to hear. And he hung up on me. But we have a great relationship! And I am not a bad mother.

For a few years in my thirties I worked for a woman who is pretty much universally regarded as a world-class slave driver. One night I was sitting behind her in a darkened room in Texas, watching a focus group. As I looked on in amazement, some underling handed her a faxed stack of papers, which happened to be her daughter's homework. Still half listening to the focus-group participants talk about our magazine, she began methodically going through the faxed sheets, correcting her daughter's work. *Oh, how sad,* I thought. If she didn't work so hard and spent more time at home, she would not have to help her daughter with homework, by fax, from halfway across the country. She would not be a bad mother.

And then one day I was on a business trip when my son's report card came out. He faxed it to my hotel, with a note and a smiley face drawn on the bottom of the page. But of course I am usually at home when the report cards come out! And I am not a bad mother.

Growing older is a humbling process, but not just because

every year you are a bit less vital and arguably less attractive than you were the year before. No, each new year brings with it the greater understanding that you are a complete idiot and hardly know anything about anything. Including working, motherhood, and what being a "good" mother really means. For many years I knew — *knew* — that I could never be the editor in chief of a magazine because it would mean I could not also be a good mother. What did I know? As it turns out, very little.

Now I work with a number of women who have children, and I wonder how they judge me as a mother. When I leave the office most nights at 5:30 to have dinner with my kids, do they think I am setting a good example, or not working hard enough? When I interrupt a meeting to take a cell phone call from my son, who is at Best Buy with our babysitter and is desperate to purchase a new Wii game and, after all, we owe him sixty dollars in allowance (yes, really, sixty dollars — and he gets only five dollars per week), are my coworkers amused or annoyed? When I send one of them an e-mail before 6:00 a.m., do they realize I am just getting work done when I can, or do they think I'm psychotic (see *E-mail — friend or foe?* p. 61)? I couldn't say, and they're certainly not going to tell me. What has worked for me may never work for them; everyone must forge her own path through the briar patch of motherhood, and you've got to find the thorns for yourself.

Last night I was at a company party with another former boss, this one a man. He was telling me that my biggest strength is also my biggest weakness, which is that I'm stubborn, I know my own mind, and I always think I have the right answer. (See *Image consultant,* p. 99.) He went on to say that people would probably describe him the same way. I disagreed; he has the benefit of more experience and knows what he doesn't know. Where motherhood is concerned—and, honestly, so, so many other things—I am still learning that lesson. With each passing year, with each new boss, with each new stage of my children's development, I know just a little bit less.

Routine exam: The evaluation you undertake when you look at your daily life and see that, week in and week out, you eat the same breakfast, sit in the same train car, walk the same route to work, have the same meetings, argue the same issues with your children, sleep on the same side of the bed.

Question: Does this qualify as a rut?

Answer: Most definitely.

Search and rescue
Self-cleaning kitchen
Separate issue
Separation anxiety
Sick in the head
Sisterhood of the black, lightweight wool pants
Spontaneous combustion
Spousal reform
Stress fracture
Stress management
Stress test
Sunday night stomp

Search and rescue: The mission you must take before any sporting event, when your son is required to be at the field "five minutes ago" and is in a panic because he and his father have "turned the house upside down" and his baseball glove/soccer shirt/lacrosse stick/helmet is "nowhere to be found," despite the fact that it was "right here by the front door" mere seconds before. And so you, the hero of the hour, calmly walk out to the driveway and find the glove/shirt/stick/helmet on the backseat of the car, where all missing clothing and sporting equipment end up, although no one seems to realize this but you.

Self-cleaning kitchen: The handy device a working mom needs in order to avoid ever having to wipe up food spills. A.k.a. the family dog.

Three months into my current job, my husband convinced me that it was the ideal time for us to adopt a puppy. Our two older boys were then eight and five, and we felt there was something missing from our little nuclear unit. Little did we know that the missing thing was actually another child (see *Accounting error,* p. 14); at the time a dog seemed like just the ticket. We both had dogs growing up and held on to idealistic notions about life with a canine, because when you are an adult thinking wistfully about your childhood pet you don't dwell on things like shedding or veterinary bills or dog crap all over your yard. Why spoil the fun? You also don't think about the fact that a big dog in a small house presents a number of problems, not the least of which is that once he is no longer a puppy, there is always a giant, hairy creature lying right in your path when you are trying to walk from one room to another. And so there are certain families, not mentioning any names, who end up having to buy a bigger house to accommodate the dog, and in that way the dog becomes extremely expensive. But I digress.

Our dog, a Labrador retriever, is named Uki, and he is a reject (a term I suspect I am not encouraged to use) from Guiding Eyes for the Blind. He was released from the program (read: rejected) at eight weeks. The explanation in his chart was that he "lacks confidence," which makes us love him all the more. Uki is a wonder, and I don't know what we will ever do when he dies, which I'm hoping never happens. He is obedient and sweet and infinitely patient. He sheds more than you could ever possibly imagine, but I'm willing to overlook that. He is up to any challenge and is extremely flexible. He is always *there,* whether you notice him or not, which is a tremendous plus. He never runs away because he knows we would die of heartbreak and he loves us too much to let that happen. He sleeps with my two older boys, which makes all three of them feel safer, and he allows the youngest to poke him in the side and lie on top of him and float toys in his water bowl. When he is being taken advantage of or ignored he just looks at me with a wise resignation that says, *This too shall pass.* Except for the shedding, he is the perfect dog.

Now, as one in a long line of Labs bred to aid the blind, he is genetically programmed to sit at your feet and wait patiently until you need him to accompany you someplace. But since everyone in our household can see, he has cleverly adapted his usefulness to suit our family's needs. Instead he just sits at your feet and waits for you to spill something edible, so he can helpfully clean it up for you. He is very, very good at this, and I know all of his Guiding Eyes forebears would be quite proud.

It took some fine-tuning for Uki to develop this skill, but, like many puppies, he showed promise at an early age. To wit: neutering day. On the morning he was scheduled to be neutered—a procedure that required his stomach to be empty—I got up early to go to the gym. Everyone else in the house was still asleep, including Uki. We kept his food in a low cabinet in the kitchen, and that morning I carefully attached a note with masking tape to the cabinet (on the miraculous off chance that someone besides me would be inspired to give him breakfast). "DO NOT FEED THE DOG," the note said. When I got home from the gym forty-five minutes later, Uki had eaten the note. And the masking tape. Plus a few Legos that were on the kitchen table. (Note: a dog stomach that contains paper, masking tape, and Legos does not qualify as empty as far as veterinarians are concerned. Yes, we had to reschedule.)

So Uki was a good eater from the start, if some of his efforts were a bit misguided. But as he grew, he gained the knowledge that pieces of cinnamon toast and steamed green beans and the occasional meatball in tomato sauce were much tastier than Legos, and therefore worth waiting for. Are there foods that Uki will not eat? Of course! At present I can only think of garlic skins, but maybe the rest will come to me. Although we deliberately do not "give" him people food, with three boys eating at once, enough food flies off the table on its own to keep Uki ever watchful. And, of course, having a baby who learns to throw food from his high chair—well, that was just about the best thing that's ever happened to Uki. Canine heaven.

There are negatives. We have to take elaborate measures to keep Uki from eating our cat's food, which is a pain. He will eat things that he shouldn't, like whole steamed artichokes, which make him throw up. He eats items out of the garbage, and goose poop at the local park, which is absolutely disgusting. And then there is a lot of pell-mell running through the house to gobble up something that has just fallen in the other room. I suspect that on one vet trip, when I was out of earshot, Uki asked for some sort of device to be implanted in his flank, so that if a piece of popcorn falls onto the kitchen floor while he is lying half-asleep in the living room, he can still detect the vibration. Because, boy, does he ever come flying into the room to take care of it. And you had better get out of the way. Did I mention that Uki weighs ninety pounds? Our toddler has not yet learned to step aside at the sound of Uki's toenails on the hardwood floor and has been knocked over more than once.

At some point he might stop throwing food off his high chair, as revenge.

But back to the working-mom benefit here. Need I say more? I don't think I've had to sweep food from our kitchen floor since 2002. That's a lot of time saved, if you add it up. When my family eats at my dogless sister's house, and there is a sprinkling of crumbs beneath the table, I look down at it in annoyance, thinking, *Why is no one coming along to eat this stuff up so I don't have to get out the broom?* I wait and wait, and the crumbs just sit there. Sad. One of the best pieces of advice I can offer any half-insane working mom, even if it seems counterintuitive and likely to create more work, is to get a dog as soon as possible. If your dog turns out to be even a quarter as sweet as Uki, you'll wonder what took you so long.

Separate issue: The children you bear who will, inevitably, spend most of their lives apart from you. And your issue? That you will never stop missing them, and there's nothing you can do about it.

On the night our third child was born, the hospital was so busy that the delivery rooms and nursery were filled to capacity, and all the staff seemed to have too much to do. After my son arrived, I spent some time in the delivery room with my husband and new baby, and then we all headed upstairs: my husband and I to my room and our son to the nursery. Hours passed. Nurses came and went, checking my blood pressure, giving me ice packs, poking at my abdomen. Eventually my husband went home. I lay in bed in the darkened room, on my back for the first time in months, staring at the framed Léger poster on the opposite wall and wondering when in the world they were going to bring my son back to me. I was exhausted, of course, but how could I sleep? I wanted to be with my child. After two hours, I rang the nurse. "Can I see my baby?" I asked. "He's coming, he's coming!" she said. Finally he did, and I never wanted to let him go.

The thrill of seeing one of my children after any absence never goes away. It doesn't matter if he has gone to the nursery for two hours or to a sleepover for one night or to camp for two solid weeks. The excitement of reuniting always surprises me, and I greet my sons with an enthusiasm that no doubt seems overplayed to them. These days when I come home from work, only our youngest responds in kind. While his older brothers glance up from what they are doing with a nonchalant "Hi, Mom," my two-year-old runs to the door with a wide-eyed "Mommy!!! Hi!!!!" It's as if he has not seen me since that first night at the hospital, and his exuberance reflects what I'm feeling inside.

On my last day of maternity leave with my first son, I sat on the sofa in our Brooklyn apartment, with my sleeping baby on my chest, and just cried. *Oh, child,* I thought, *you have no idea how I'm going to fail you.* We were just getting to know each other. I imagined all the ways in which I was not going to be there for him, sharing the small joys and disappointments that make up most of life. We were both venturing into the great unknown that was our new family, and I would not always be by his side. I did this complicated calculation, adding up all the hours that our babysitter would be spending with our son during the week versus the time I would spend with him. I wanted to prove to myself that I had not fully given my child over to someone else, that I was with him more than 50 percent of the time, that I was still the primary caregiver. That no matter who she was, I would always be Mommy.

On my last day of maternity leave with my second son, I thought it was important that we do something special, meaningful, memorable, as a family. I planned a trip to a little aquarium about an hour from our house. We got a late start, hit traffic on the way, and didn't have much time before the aquarium closed. I was tense; no one had a lot of fun. On the way back we hit even more traffic, and I stared glumly out the window, counting the minutes of the afternoon as they passed into evening. That time, more than sadness, what I felt was anger at myself: I abandoned my children every day and I couldn't even get it right when I was home.

I don't remember the last day of maternity leave with my third son, even though it was the most recent. By that time, more than a decade after my first maternity leave, I knew not to make too much of it; the more importance you attach to an event, the greater your chances for disappointment. I also had become accustomed to the sadness of separation.

Before I had children, I imagined myself and my future offspring like a mother duck and her ducklings: navigating our way through a big scary world together, united, following the same path. Once I had children, it didn't take me long to realize that separation would define much of motherhood.

Now I have come to regard my relationship with each of my kids as if we were pairs skaters: we come together and then move apart, with convergence and independence, following an elaborate routine that we both know. We may be a team, but every hello has a good-bye right behind it.

After more than a decade of working motherhood, I have hit many pockets of sadness. Some I have worked through, and some I will be stuck in forever. For example, I have passed through the sad fear that any babysitter can take my place in the hearts and minds of my children. But I will never get over the sting of separation, or the knowledge that the times of separation grow as my children get older. Years go by and, like a brilliant longtime pair of skaters, my children and I adapt our routine. We understand each other's roles without having to define them. I will continue to miss them, no matter how much time passes. And whenever they call "Mommy?" (or, later, "Mom?"), they will be calling for me. I wish I could always be there to hear it.

Separation anxiety: When everyone else is at the office and you aren't, the fear you feel that you are going to be fired or demoted or at the very least completely forgotten. This fear is especially pronounced when you take a one-week vacation (see *Vacation algorithm,* p. 223). However, even working from home on a single Friday may set off an entire weekend of paranoia that lingers until it is replaced by the heaviness of heart you feel when you go to work on Monday morning and realize that, unfortunately, you still have a job.

Sick in the head: Your state when you are suffering from any make-believe, stress-induced disease — that is, the illness of an overextended mom with an active imagination.

Perhaps you suspect — just a bit — that you have Guillain-Barré syndrome or hypothyroidism because you are so tired all the time. Or maybe you are slightly convinced that your little cough is actually typhoid, which you will eventually die of (leaving your family bereft as they finally realize all the things you did to keep the household running smoothly, such as throw out the oranges that have gone mushy but that no one else seems to notice in the bottom of the fruit drawer). Just today I woke up at 5:10 with sharp pains in my stomach. Now, it could be an ulcer or a ruptured appendix. Really! Or it could just be stress.

Sisterhood of the black, lightweight wool pants: The tribe of working mothers who are united in their reliance upon the just-right pair of pants that can be worn for three seasons, at least once a week, year in and year out.

Spontaneous combustion: An unexpected and violent — in fact, often uncontrollable — eruption of tears brought on by some seemingly innocuous event. The likelihood of spontaneous combustion occurring on any given day is almost entirely governed by level of well-restedness and hormonal state.

One day my friend Mimi was dropping her son off at nursery school. Mimi's husband is a stay-at-home dad (see *Dudley Do-Everything,* p. 55), and he usually does the nursery school drop-off. But on this day the task fell to Mimi, which was exciting to both her and her son. However, something startling happened when she was saying good-bye: she began crying and couldn't stop. Then her son started crying and couldn't stop either. They crouched in the hall, clutching each other, weeping, when a doctor friend happened upon them.

Let me pause for a moment to mention that Mimi had been using the birth control patch, which had recently come off. So her hormonal situation was...well...anybody's guess. The doctor friend took one look at Mimi and said, "What is wrong with you!? Are you off your patch?"

The moral of this story: before spontaneous combustion causes you to question your entire existence, check your exhaustion level. And don't forget your hormones.

Spousal reform: A process of husband rehabilitation that requires meetings into the night to try to address such problems as the lack of concern about kids' bedtimes, the refusal to answer the phone even though he is closer to it than you are, and dozens of subtopics related to who is responsible for dinner.

Stress fracture: The break that occurs when your blood pressure is going through the roof and no one around you sees it, hears it, or seems to care even the tiniest bit.

Apparently stress is a necessary factor in life; without stress there would be no fight-or-flight impulse, for example. Without stress new presidents who promise to save our country would never be elected, divorce lawyers would go out of business, and no one would have invented Lexapro. For working moms, stress can take on a motivational speaker role: it's the force that pushes you out of bed in the morning to get things done. But as part of the fabric of your daily life, stress most often takes the shape of "Why am I running around like a maniac while everyone else watches ESPN?" And that is a *stress fracture.*

The key stress fracture in my life happens every morning from 7:15 to 8:40, when the three individuals who have the hardest time getting out the door are moving at radically different speeds: I am a Ferrari, my middle son is a unicycle, and my husband is a hearse. It's an action-packed, bruising race in which we need to get everybody dressed and fed and out of the house, and it all leads up to the make-or-break moment: the dash for the commuter train.

My husband and I take the train together, so in theory we can lovingly share sections of the paper, brainstorm solutions to family problems, and commiserate about work issues, all of which will bring us closer together as a modern-day, time-pressed, hardworking parental unit. Which we would be if it weren't for one major incompatibility: I like to arrive at the station five minutes before the train is due and I am married to a man who likes to arrive as the train is pulling into the station. If I had a dollar for every time I have sprinted from my car to the train as the doors stood open — sometimes with tissues flying out of the pocket of my coat, which makes for a particularly charming and sophisticated look — I'd have enough money to retire for life, and maybe even *buy* ESPN. In the twelve years we've lived in the suburbs, we've missed the train more times than I can possibly count. But on the days we make it — which,

I'll admit, is most days—my husband will look at me as we jump onto the train with an expression that says: *Doesn't it make you feel alive?!* And I return his wild-eyed grin with a glare that says, *Actually, it makes me want to kill you.* Luckily, by the time we see each other at the end of the day my stress fracture has healed, and so the next morning it can happen all over again.

Stress management: A boss who leads with fear, not encouragement; who talks without listening; who makes demands without explanations; who insults you in public when a private conversation would do; who does not acknowledge a personal life; who constantly changes his mind; who can't make a decision; who micromanages your every move; who second-guesses your every decision; who makes you feel like an inconvenience; who eventually forces you to say, "I am leaving, because you are not worth it."

Stress test: The self-analysis you must undergo when you are acting like a completely unbearable person. The test consists of one question: Is there something deeply wrong with me, or has stress taken over?

Sunday night stomp: A dance-cum-tantrum first identified by my friend Elizabeth, hardworking mother of four. The SNS is performed generally by the mom and generally between the hours of 5:00 p.m. and 10:00 p.m. Length of dance, specific steps, and intensity of performance vary week by week, depending on how much of her weekend to-do list she did not accomplish.

Take Halloween, for example

Technological bipolarism

That-sounds-like-fun-I'll-try-it!

Theater of the absurd

Time management

TMI

To-do haiku

Triumph of the caregiver

Take Halloween, for example: A phrase that is like a secret handshake for working moms — the indication that you understand the unique and seemingly benign events that thrill your children and fill you with nothing but dread.

If it is true about parenting that the years are short but the days are long, well, certain days are about twice as long as others. Beginning with Halloween, which is hands down my least favorite day of the year. Any twenty-four-hour period that combines costumes, parades, children running loose around the neighborhood with unlimited candy (in the dark, no less), extended bedtimes, and strangers ringing your doorbell every fifteen minutes is one worth dreading. It is no accident that last Halloween I cut my thumb making chili and bled so much and for so long that I made my husband come home from work to tell me if I needed stitches. We called our friend who is an emergency room doctor on his cell phone to get his opinion and accidentally woke him up, because he happened to be in Sri Lanka. Of course — why wouldn't he be? It was

Halloween. And can't somebody do something about October 31 frequently falling on a workday? It's just really...inconvenient. I know I am not alone among mothers in my hatred of Halloween, because I have discussed this with anyone who will listen. I also know I am not alone in my dread of field trips that involve buses, and slumber parties held at my house. But I try to put on a good face and enthusiastically participate in Halloween, field trips, and slumber parties, for the sake of my children. And when they become parents themselves and marvel at how awful days like these are, I can say, *I know exactly what you mean.*

Technological bipolarism: When you wake up in the morning and can't imagine how you would get through life without your BlackBerry, but by bedtime you want to strap a bomb to it and blow it to smithereens.

That-sounds-like-fun-I'll-try-it!: A very, very dangerous train of thought that, if ridden to the end of the line, may very well result in some sort of crash. If you are an adventurous sort, as I apparently am, you mistakenly believe that you should take on more than you sensibly can handle. This attitude leads to a cavalier "oh, what the hell" approach to life that results in involvement in all sorts of community boards, business mentoring programs, and other activities you'd be better off avoiding. In a word: *overextension.* The overextension impulse is at its root a good one, and it leads to moments like the one I had in the grocery store a few weeks back when an extremely accomplished, slightly older, and sort of scary working mom I know told me, "I don't know how you do it!" The only proper response to such a remark is to humbly deflect the observation and not dwell on it too much, because dwelling on it will result in conceit or the horrifying realization that you actually *can't* do it, in which case you might go into cardiac arrest in the canned food aisle (see *Ignore the tray,* p. 99).

That-sounds-like-fun-I'll-try-it! describes the exact moments that add up to an existence that is wonderful, fun, challenging, blessed, and just a bit too full. In my life, That-sounds-like-fun-I'll-try-it! has precipitated the following:

- Moving to New York City
- Running a magazine
- Having a baby when my oldest child was approaching puberty
- Doing an extensive home renovation while still living in the house
- Hand-washing sweaters
- Buying too many houseplants and insisting on trying to keep them all alive
- Getting a puppy and a new job at the same time
- Making red velvet cake from scratch
- Sewing curtains

Theater of the absurd: Your nightly attempt to tell stories about your day that are interesting enough to hold the attention of your bored and skeptical children.

I have this belief, perhaps mistaken, that it is beneficial to the family that my children know a little bit about Mom's working life: they will see that it is possible — despite countless sitcom examples to the contrary — to be a grown-up and like your job; they will learn that work life has its ups and downs; and hearing more about my day will encourage them to tell me more about theirs. (This last part, p.s., will never happen, in part because I gave birth to three boys instead of three girls. To hear my own mother tell it, at our family dinner table you couldn't get anybody to shut up).

My boys are polite much of the time and unless I've just told them that we're never going to get an Xbox or insist that they feed the cat, they treat me and my husband with kindness and respect. And so at dinnertime when I trot out stories about my day, they feign interest for as long as possible (that is, about forty seconds). I have found, however, that there are certain key themes that my children find endlessly fascinating, most of them things that simply serve to underscore the absurdity of working with other people and humankind in general. (Think *Waiting for Guffman*, the magazine version.)

Themes that never fail to hold my children's interest:

- Anyone who is out to get me
- Coworkers who are mean, to me or anyone else
- Anyone getting fired, either by me or someone else
- Anybody crying in the office
- Any meeting that has to be held in secret

- Any giant raise or promotion, if it involves someone they have met
- Any time I "get in trouble" with my boss

In the absence of one of these themes, exaggeration must come into play. I once described a man who worked in another division of my company as "the most boring man in the world." One day I had lunch with him and discovered that he was not boring at all; he was quite interesting once you got to know him a bit. Thereafter he became known by my middle son—who was about five at the time—as "the most boring man in the world who is not boring." Because his identity was so fascinating and easy for a five-year-old to grasp, the most boring–not boring man became a major character in my theater of the absurd, even though he was at best a minor character in my real working life. A couple of years after our lunch, "the most boring man in the world who is not boring" left the company; I'm still not quite ready to tell my children.

Time management: What?

TMI: The things about your coworkers that you don't want to know because the information makes you uncomfortable, squeamish, or bored. These topics include most surgeries, most vacations, most child achievements, most pet problems. (Always up for discussion: babysitter issues, terrible behavior on the part of other mothers at school, lazy husbands.)

To-do haiku: The list of tasks or semi-important things to remember that replays like a song stuck in your head until you finally find a pen and write it down. For example:

Pick up dry cleaning
Where are my black boots? At work?
Did we pay that bill?

To-do haiku are also useful for some of life's bigger issues:

How is my marriage?
Do I even like this job?
Does my ass look fat?

Triumph of the caregiver: When children injure themselves (or damage valuable property, or get into physical fights, or just generally make really bad decisions) not on your babysitter's watch, but on yours.

As a working mother, your biggest fear — maybe the only real fear — is that something horrible will happen to your children when you are at work. You can't dwell on this without making yourself crazy. I have learned to bury this fear (see *Leap of faith,* p. 125), in part because all of the scary and dramatic injuries that have befallen my children have happened when either my husband or I was "in charge." Just a few examples:

- Our middle son needed two stitches next to his eye after he tripped on the rug in our bedroom.
- Our oldest son needed three stitches on the back of his head when he fell on the tile in the shower.
- Our middle son needed thirty-two (!) stitches over his eye after he fell onto the edge of a cabinet while trying to put a Green Day disc into the CD player. He also bled all over his Incredible Hulk T-shirt, which to him was the bigger problem.
- Our middle son (is there a pattern here?) broke his ankle while jumping off our front porch.
- Our middle son (yes, definitely a pattern) almost got hit by a car when he ran out into the street in front of our local bike shop.
- An eight-year-old family friend fell off a cliff in our backyard.
- Our oldest son put his hand in a candle flame at his first birthday party.
- Our youngest put his hand in a Sterno flame at a street fair.

I can say with both shame and relief that in the fourteen years we have employed other people to take care of our children while we were at work, there has not been a single incident with a babysitter that involved stitches, broken bones, or a trip to the emergency room. The worst thing that ever happened on a babysitter's watch was the dog running away, and

I think he was gone for all of an hour and a half. Clearly I am not as vigilant a parent as I might be; I am also very lucky in my choice of babysitters. Which leads me to wonder: if someone actually paid me to be a parent (not in personal fulfillment and a lifetime of hugs, but in cold hard cash), would my safety record improve?

Undercompensating
Unhappy hour
Unmilestones
Usual suspects
Utter nonsense

Undercompensating: The necessary mode of survival for many working mothers.

In order to master undercompensating, first you must eliminate any *overcompensating* tendencies common in young working moms (see *Guilt curve,* p. 83). If you play your cards right, the drive to overcompensate will all but disappear by the time your oldest child hits middle school. That's when you get really clever and begin to understand that as a working mother who is rarely around during the day you can rely heavily — in fact, more than you should — on the stay-at-home mothers who like and maybe pity you a bit and are willing to pull more than their weight when it comes to things like class parties, collecting money for teacher gifts, and figuring out if the school lunch menu is nutritious enough. I've found that if you just write a yearly check to the PTA and sponsor some sort of ride at the annual school carnival, you can make yourself believe that you are participating.

Unhappy hour: The sixty minutes immediately following your return from work when you kick off your uncomfortable shoes and put your feet up, regaling your spouse with amusing and triumphant stories from your day as he mixes your martini and—

Whoops, wrong life.

The sixty minutes immediately following your return from work when the baby is crying because he wants to go outside and your middle child is whining because he doesn't want to empty the dishwasher and your oldest child is completely AWOL. There is no putting your feet up and there is no martini, only a pair of nutty parents who insist on eating dinner with the kids every night because years ago they read someplace that eating dinner as a family will prevent their children from becoming heroin addicts. And, seriously, that had better be the case, because eighteen years is a long time to go without a happy hour.

Unmilestones: Important developmental moments in the lives of your children that no one notices but that, regarded as a whole, present the depressing truth that your kids are growing up and away from you.

A couple of weeks ago I was giving our two-year-old a bath and my eleven-year-old got in the tub with him. As I watched the two of them together, I realized that there was a time not long ago when my eleven-year-old and I would bathe together, but that time seems to have ended. I did not get the memo from my son that he would no longer be bathing with me, but apparently he composed one and is following through. Our last bath — which I did not note as important at the time, and which I now do not remember — was an unmilestone: a transitional moment that passes without you realizing it until it is too late to celebrate (or, more likely, to mourn).

There are a number of things I am good at where motherhood is concerned, but sustained listening or, for that matter, really paying attention is not one of them. Here is a typical interaction between me and one of my sons, from the other night:

Me: How was soccer practice, honey?

Kid: It was *terrible.*

Me: Oh! That's too bad. Was it becau — Hey, if you want some juice, would you mind taking it out of the bottle in the fridge instead of drinking a juice box?

Kid: OK, sure.

Me: Thanks, sweetie.

And then we both go our separate ways. There have been all sorts of studies about how multitasking is counterproductive, that we as a society can no longer really focus on anything, blah blah blah. Working motherhood is nothing if not the ultimate triumph of multitasking over sustained focus. Because I am always doing five things at once, I am never really present. Short of becoming a Buddhist, I'm not quite sure how to change.

And so I wonder: is this why I can't remember the last time I took a bath with my eleven-year-old, because I'm never really *there,* but merely visiting? I wish someone (hello, Buddha?) would institute a system in which a pleasant chime rings whenever an event that you're eventually going to want to remember is happening. You know, the way certain highways have a strip of serrated pavement that makes a hideous noise if you start driving off the edge? Something like that, just more melodious.

Part of the reason people have more children is to relive the moments they weren't paying much attention to the last time around. This morning I lifted our two-year-old into bed beside my husband, and he patted my pillow insistently, saying, "Mommy! *Mommy!*" to let me know that he wanted me to join them. He is at such an incredibly sweet age; I really could just stare at him all day long and be perfectly content. As I climbed into bed next to him, I thought to myself, I *will* remember this. Of course I won't. There's just too much other stuff in my head, and between my to-do list, work concerns, and trivia from bizarre news items I've recently read, there's very little space left for important moments.

One of the best and worst things about being a parent is that your children will continue to grow, with or without you noting every step. One of the best — and worst — things about being a working mom is that you're not always focused on that process. The unmilestones are happening all around you, every day of the week. When my two-year-old uses a sippy cup for the very last time, I may be sitting in a meeting in my office, discussing what to shoot for the cover (or perhaps just what to eat for lunch). The moment will pass, and I will be completely unaware of it. Until the day a few months later when I will think to myself, *Hey, when did the sippy cup go away?* And then I'll want nothing more than to be able to hit rewind, in an effort to acknowledge the moment, just this once.

Usual suspects: The panel of forces you must consider before you commit to having a full-blown working-mother existential crisis. Before you allow yourself to question your entire life and any decision you have ever made, check: hormones, sleep deprivation level, messiness of house, whining level of children, ridiculousness of colleagues. If none of these is the guilty party responsible for your unhappiness, then you may indeed have bigger problems.

Utter nonsense: Those things you say at home when your mind is still at work. The most common example is calling one child by another child's name. Then there is calling the dog by a child's name, which I do from time to time. Finally there is inserting a completely irrelevant word into a sentence: "Why, we'd love to come to dinner on Saturday night! I don't think we have any other plans. Let me just check the budget."

Vacation algorithm
Vanishing act
Very, verrryyyyy sleeeeeepy . . .
Vision quest
Visitor's pass to your own life
Voodoo economics

Vacation algorithm: The process by which you achieve your own personal maximum relaxation level. Through the following series of steps, you use the vacation algorithm to reach a place of satisfaction and contentment, where your self-definition has nothing to do with your work.

Step 1: Vacation begins. You miss work; you're stressed; you feel an overwhelming need to return to your "normal" life (see *Separation anxiety,* p. 198).

Step 2: A couple of days in. While you're not missing work, you are stressed nonetheless; need to return to "normal" life.

Step 3: Vacation halfway over. You're not missing work; not stressed; vaguely remember "normal" life as somewhat appealing.

Step 4: Last day of vacation. You're not missing work, in fact not thinking about work at all; not stressed; never want to go back to "normal" life for as long as you live.

Now, how you apply the vacation algorithm depends on your job status, temperament, and, most important, the amount of time you are able to take off. I was forty years old before I realized that I could not separate my sense of self from my job without taking two full weeks in a row. Anything less than that, and I never completely feel like I am on vacation. If you are more highly evolved than I am, you can probably rediscover yourself in a much shorter period of time, maybe even over a weekend.

Vanishing act: The fantasy-life maneuver in which you suddenly disappear. Here's how mine goes: I tell the family that I am going to the grocery store and take nothing with me but my wallet. (Lightness of load is essential to the vanishing act; after all, it is your heavy load that you're fleeing.) Halfway to the store, with a dramatic squeal of tires, I turn and get onto I-95. I drive and drive and drive: the destination is not important; it's what I've left behind that counts.

Very, verrryyyyy sleeeeeeepy...: Your constant state. No hypnosis required.

One evening a few winters back I was riding my commuter train after work, minding my own business, wishing the ride would last a bit longer so I could finish the paper and have twenty more minutes to myself (see *Palate cleanser,* p. 163). As the doors opened at Mount Vernon, the first stop on the line, there was a great commotion in the seat in front of me. Apparently its occupant had fallen asleep and was about to miss his stop. Flustered, he rushed to gather his things as the rest of us silently cheered him on, hoping we would not hear the bell signal that the doors were going to close before he could get out. With lots of huffing and grunting and coat dragging, he made it through the train and leaped onto the cold platform. *Hooray!* we all thought. *The triumph of a fellow commuter!* Then he opened his mouth. "Is this Larchmont!?" he gasped.

That is why I do not fall asleep on the train. Under the right circumstances, however, I could fall asleep at any time of day, any day of the week (see "*Just let me lie down,*" p. 112). There was nothing in the manual for adulthood that warned me about constant exhaustion, but it should have been a whole chapter. I am always tired, and one of the most boring things about me is that I talk about it incessantly. One year my husband and I made a joint New Year's resolution: we were not allowed to complain about how tired we were, because we are much better people than that. I think it lasted a day and a half. I have no doubt that I'm the one who broke it first. In fact, if God came down and told me that I was no longer allowed to complain about the messy state of our house, my children's deplorable dental hygiene, how I can never get through my e-mail, or how tired I am, I think I would be silent 70 percent of the time. There really is very little else to talk about.

I sometimes wonder if I would be so tired if I were not working. Or would I then just volunteer for every committee that came my way, and before you know it I'd be hunched over my sewing machine at 2:00 a.m., making Oompa-Loompa costumes for the local children's theater? Who's to say? But because I am working, I blame the job for my constant exhaustion. Besides the fact that trying so hard to get along with other people is incredibly tiring, work also takes up a giant portion of your day when you could otherwise be enjoying a nap. And the kids! The other thing the adulthood manual did not mention was that once you have a child in middle school, he has to get up at 6:20 every day and you'd better be in charge of that, sister, because even a brass band could not get that boy out of bed. So forget about ever staying up until 11:30 on a school night. And then there are the things that are just too painful to discuss: babies who cry out at ungodly hours, eleven-year-olds who wander into your room with itchy feet and need Aquaphor ASAP, husbands who snore, boys who argue in the middle of the night about who gets to sleep with the dog. This is just life, everything you signed up for when you got married and had kids and held on to your fulfilling career. You just didn't know when you signed up that you were signing away all rights to be well rested too.

My father was a fairly heavy smoker for decades until the nagging of his loved ones finally got to him, and he abruptly quit. Years later I asked him if he missed smoking. "Every single day," he replied. And so I think about sleep in the way I imagine my father thinks about cigarettes: that is, constantly and with extreme longing. Every single day.

Vision quest: Your lifelong search for a path, a direction, an assemblage of patterns, a plan: anything to indicate that the apparently random and haphazard way you have of choosing jobs and raising children (see *The X Factor,* p. 241) is part of a larger vision. Which you—being a visionary—have known all along.

Visitor's pass to your own life: The imaginary permission slip you need to engage in certain nonwork activities. Think about it: You may have every right to take some time away from work and spend a Tuesday morning at the mall. Or leave the office at lunch to pick your daughter up from school. And yet these activities are so removed from your daily routine that you feel like an intruder in your own life. If you just had a visitor's pass, you could pin it to your shirt and prove to all of the regulars that you belong.

Voodoo economics: The ongoing hocus-pocus calculation that you must make to determine which to prioritize on any given day: your time or your money. There is really no specific formula. It should be noted that voodoo economics (and not rank stupidity) leads certain people to buy closet storage bins at Target without measuring the height of the closet shelves first, and then put them in the basement, unused, when they don't fit on the shelves, because just the thought of having to negotiate customer service at Target is too much to bear, financial loss be damned.

Wardrobe malfunction
"Who moved my cheese?"
Wine imperative
The winker
Women not on the verge of a nervous breakdown
Working motherhood according to Sisyphus
Workplace 101
Work release
A wrinkle in time

Wardrobe malfunction: When your carefully planned career-appropriate look goes terribly awry.

Over the years, friends have shared some doozy wardrobe malfunctions: the time Janet wore two different shoes to work, one black and one navy, and didn't notice until she was at an important lunch with her boss and a client; the time Kim's son pulled on her skirt during elementary school drop-off and the entire thing slid to the floor, revealing her thonged derriere to the first-grade class. I've had my own truly embarrassing malfunctions, including the time, when my third son was a newborn, that my nursing pad leaked through my silk shirt while I was firing someone in my office. That was uniquely humiliating.

Then there was the Grand Central Shoe Debacle. I was working at *Vogue* magazine, where high heels were an occupational requirement. Because my midtown Manhattan office was right across the street from Grand Central Station, I was spared the silly *Working Girl* habit of changing into flats or — horrors — sneakers when I left the office; instead I could actually commute in high heels. (I was also young and reckless then, and my calf muscles were a bit more up to the challenge.) On this particular day I was wearing black pumps with a two-inch heel that were perhaps a half size too big. As I clomped down the platform toward my commuter train, I could hear someone closing in on me. When I stepped onto the train, this someone accidentally kicked the back of my foot and my shoe flew off, sailing into the gap between the platform and the train itself.

"My shoe!" I exclaimed.

My hapless fellow commuter didn't realize what had happened and seemed annoyed to be stopped. "I'm sorry," he mumbled.

"It's under the train!" I said. I held up my stockinged foot, balancing in front of him like a flamingo. Immediately he became very flustered and apologetic. "Oh!" he said. "Er — do you want my shoe?" I politely declined and hobbled to my seat, simultaneously irritated, bemused, surprised, and grateful that for once I would have a story about my day that would hold my children's interest (see *Theater of the absurd,* p. 207). And it did: for years afterward, whenever we took the kids through Grand Central, my oldest son would say, "Mommy, do you think we'll find your shoe?"

"Who moved my cheese?" The thing you shout out when you are in the kitchen on a Sunday afternoon, making lasagna (enough to provide leftovers for a couple of days), and the shredded mozzarella that you bought the day before is gone. Who ate it? Husband? Child? Visiting teenage boy? It's anybody's guess.

Other accusatory phrases you may use on a weekly basis:

- "Who has mud on his shoes?"
- "Who left the front door open?"
- "Who took the earbuds from my iPod?"
- "Who made such a mess of the microwave?"
- "Who used the rest of the toilet paper and didn't refill it?"
- "Who left this wet towel on the floor?"

You shout these things in the vain hope that someone, anyone really, will come forward and confess to making your complicated life even more complicated. Chances are, however, you get no response.

Wine imperative: The reason there is a liquor store in every large commuter rail station and a functioning bar car in any self-respecting commuter train. Next project: getting all bottles to come with a screw top.

The winker: A particular sort of man who harbors unresolved feelings about women in the workplace in general and powerful women in the workplace in particular. This inner turmoil about the need to treat women as professional equals and all that bothersome modern nonsense causes him to do odd things in meetings, like wink when you are making a presentation. A few suggestions on how to respond: ignore him; wink back; lean in uncomfortably close and say, "Do you have something in your eye? My son's entire class has conjunctivitis!"

Women not on the verge of a nervous breakdown: The rare working moms among us who are in charge of every committee and board and project and task force and who still have time to run marathons and make birthday cakes from scratch.

There are many things in life I will never understand, even if I live to be 150 years old: why umbrellas always break after six months; why tampons are so expensive; why people think *Curb Your Enthusiasm* is funny. And why a level of activity and accomplishment that seems insurmountable for some working moms is just business as usual for others.

Take my friend Mary. Mary has seven kids—OK, I could just stop there. But she also works as a lawyer for a pharmaceutical company, is on the board of our local children's theater, is the treasurer of the travel soccer program, and does the income tax returns every year for multiple members of her family. Did I mention that two of her kids are twins and three are adopted? Mary and her husband have a house in my town and a house in the country, which means that, in addition to managing seven kids and a career, she has two homes to maintain. And the one in the country has a pond, meaning there is always the possibility that someone will drown, the prevention of which is like another full-time job. Mary also has two dogs. On top of all that, she is about the nicest person you are ever going to meet, partly because she always laughs at your jokes, which makes her doubly likable. She is constantly doing something for somebody else. One night at our book club meeting Mary was saying how she had slept only three hours the night before because she was putting songs on her iPod for a soccer party that day. And she was actually smiling. I, of course, wanted to lie down under the table after just hearing the story. It was then that I knew the truth: Mary and I are not members of the same species. We may share certain physical characteristics — two arms and two legs, for example — and a common habitat. But basically Mary is a spider monkey and I'm a three-toed sloth. Sure, we both live in the trees, but that's where the similarities end.

After years of pondering what makes someone like Mary possible, I have come up with three factors: one, as I mentioned, is that Mary needs very little sleep. Two, she is married to a man who also needs very little sleep, and he is helpful in the extreme. (See *Dudley Do-Everything,* p. 55.) And three, Mary is not bedeviled by the daily speed bumps that take up so much time and energy for mere mortals like me, and just about anyone else who is not Mary. When she has a task in front of her — whether it is completing her nephew's income tax returns or painting the sets for this year's production of *Mulan Jr.* — Mary does not bitch and moan and procrastinate and think of the hundreds of things she'd like to be doing instead. She simply starts working and gets the job done, because Mary is a Doer.

Me? If I had just one day of Mary's activities, I would have to feign an extreme mental problem, something so severe that

I would be committed to an institution, where someone else could do the meal planning and make my bed for the rest of my life. Absent that, I'd love to be a genius so I could invent some kind of pill that would turn me into Mary. Imagine a country full of Marys! Our productivity would be through the roof and no one would ever complain about having to take the stairs instead of the elevator.

Of course, for every Mary there are scores of women who do not put a high premium on productivity. I appear (as always) to reside someplace in the middle, which is (as always) both a disappointment and a comfort. I am not Mary, but I can juggle family, career, and a few extracurriculars without yelling at my loved ones more than once or twice a day. When I was in high school I had a part-time job at a drugstore called Happy Harry's. The store manager was a nice guy who always treated me like an adult instead of the dreamy sixteen-year-old I was, which in turn made me a model employee. What started as a summer job became too much to handle once school started, and eventually I had to quit. When I told the manager, he tried to talk me out of leaving, saying that it was the people who are able to handle a lot who are always able to take on more.

I've thought about the manager's observation ever since, in the context of dealing with my own life, dealing with other people in my career, and dealing with women like Mary. It's true: the people at work who are the busiest tend to be busy because they are the most capable, which leads to more work and more busyness. Same for moms: the women who are the most involved in the goings-on at school and in town are rarely on just one committee or board; they are on none, or they are on five. And of the five, they are the chairmen of three.

Of course, there is the possibility that Mary and all women like her are just androids. That has occurred to me more than once.

Working motherhood according to Sisyphus:

- Once you get the laundry folded, there are three more loads to wash.
- Once you decide you like your boss, your company is restructured and you get a new one.
- The instant school is over for the summer, you've got to get everybody ready for sleepaway camp.
- As soon as the Halloween candy is finally consumed, the Christmas candy starts to arrive.
- Once you finally get your son to brush his teeth before bed, he announces that he's hungry.
- As soon as you start a workout program, you get a really bad cold and can't exercise for three weeks.
- As soon as you hire a new employee, someone else quits.

Workplace 101: The guidebook that someone should have written by now but that doesn't seem to exist. Part Miss Manners and part Machiavelli, this guide to the appropriate response to any workplace situation would include such puzzlers as "What do you do when you've used your breast pump during your lunch hour and forgotten to zip up your dress afterward?" and "How do you respond when you see your married boss on a date with a coworker?"

Work release: The feeling of gratitude and relaxation you experience at the end of a hard day when you walk in the front door of your house and into the bosom of a family that not only cannot fire you, but will not hesitate to tell you when the back of your hair looks funny or you have food in your teeth.

A wrinkle in time: When your schedule is so undone by your children's weekend activities that you don't look at your Monday calendar until you are on your way to work that morning, and it is only then that you see that you have an event to attend at lunch, an awards ceremony as a matter of fact, one you completely forgot about. Perhaps it's even at the Waldorf-Astoria hotel, and instead of a fancy outfit you are wearing blue cotton pants and a silk blouse that doesn't quite match. Not that that has ever happened to me.

The X Factor
X files
X marks the spot

The X Factor: The undefinable, wonderful something that governs the direction of your life because, let's face it, you're not really in charge.

Once upon a time, during the summer between sophomore and junior years of college, I had an internship on Capitol Hill, in the office of Senator Bill Roth. That summer provided me with a number of lasting lessons: first, that boys who act crazy in love with you might just be crazy, period; that other boys who act unattainable usually are just that; and that working as a Senate subcommittee member seems really, really boring. But one of the most interesting lessons of the summer was that not everyone on this planet lacks direction the way I do. Senator Roth made it a point to have a brief meeting with each intern at the beginning of his or her service, and I remember nothing about our chat except that he said he had wanted to be a U.S. senator since the age of eight. Eight! This fact was incomprehensible to me then, and is incomprehensible to me now, probably because I still don't know what I want to be when I grow up.

If you decide what you want to be when you are eight, there are two significant problems. One: What if you never achieve your goal? Does that make you a complete failure? And two: How do you make room for fate and serendipity?

Despite the intermittent suspicion that I should have some sort of grand plan (see *Vision quest,* p. 226), fate and serendipity have governed the path of my life. For example, my job search efforts have never been particularly focused or discriminating. Actually, that's not true: I tried repeatedly to get a job at Friendly's when I was a teenager. It was the only place I wanted to work, and I could never get hired. Which was terribly disappointing at the time, but I suppose it *built character,* as Mom always liked to point out, much to my annoyance. Once I started working in magazines, it seems jobs picked me before I even had a chance to formulate an opinion. Sometimes the jobs were wonderful and sometimes they were terrible, but it was never I who made them happen; it was serendipity.

I certainly never set out to give birth to three boys. As I write this, I live in a household with a husband, three sons, a male dog, and a male cat. I am the only female thing around. (Except for the fish—they seem to multiply.) But to be surrounded by so many penises was never the plan. It just kept happening, and I felt powerless to do anything about it. I love my three boys. Sometimes I do not love *having* three boys: there is no sitting still, which leads to chaos, which leads to destruction. That is, until an eleven-year-old girl comes over and has a perplexing, deal-breaker hissy fit about some slight that neither I nor my children even noticed. Then I am extremely grateful that I have three boys. Thank you, fate.

There is something beautiful in trusting your future to serendipity and fate, just like there is something beautiful in having a prescription for Percocet, whether or not you ever use it. Thirty years later, my answer to Senator Roth is that, as a working mom, there was no way for me to find out what I really wanted to do with myself without a significant amount of trial and error. It's the Chutes and Ladders approach to life: if you play long enough, you will make it to the end of the game board, but there is certainly a lot of backsliding along the way.

If my life had gone according to "plan," I would be living in Delaware, working as an engineer for DuPont. That was the future my parents mapped out, because presumably that's what Delaware girls who did well in high school math and science grew up to be. I never actively rebelled against this plan, unless you call getting terrible grades in college math and science a rebellion. I just let the tide carry me to majoring in English, which carried me to graduate school, which brought me to New York City, where I eventually landed in magazines. I've ended up running a big enterprise (how did *that* happen?) and having three boys (whose idea was *that?*), and because I've never set any particular direction for myself, I never know if I'm lost. Which is actually sort of nice.

X files: A system (maybe it's alphabetical, or color coded, or chronological—you've heard all sorts of rumors, and they all sound equally unbelievable) that working mothers of the mysteriously highly organized variety apparently employ to keep it all together. Being a garden-variety working mother, you do not have your children's immunization records all filed together in a home office drawer, or the warranties of your appliances in a handy little binder above the kitchen phone. You do not have all of your children's school photos filed by year (see *Quest through the chaos,* p. 177), nor do you have a fire safe in the basement with everybody's birth certificates in it. It is important that you not let your lack of a superior filing system make you feel insecure; your inability to achieve this level of organization does not make you an inferior creature, just human.

X marks the spot: The imaginary end of the imaginary treasure map you wish existed for all the times — that is, about a dozen every day — when your child claims he can't find something that is either right in front of him, lost in the disaster zone that is his bedroom, or left in his locker at school. Because you were not the one to last lay eyes on the lost object, and because the maximum time any child can spend looking for something before giving up is approximately ninety seconds, a helpful treasure map with a clearly marked X would not only make your life run more efficiently, but would turn the loathsome process of searching for lost items into a semipleasurable game the whole family might enjoy.

Yesterday's news
Young and restless
Your Non-Retirement Retirement,
    an Owner's Manual

Yesterday's news: What you will be if you don't mind your p's and q's and you allow yourself to become old.

Being old is not the same thing as aging. Being old is avoidable, whereas aging is not. And it's not about appearance; it's about the way you think. There is nothing more depressing than a woman clinging so hard to some youthful ideal that she has plastic surgeried herself into another species. And just because she looks like a twenty-one-year-old alien does not mean that she is young on the inside. Right now, for example, although I wear the same dress size I did ten years ago, I am in grave danger of becoming old because I do not know how to send a text message from my cell phone. No one else my age seems to have this problem. My teenage son has twice, and with great patience, tried to teach me how to send a text. And still I forget. This may be a sign that I am just not very interested in texting, or it may be that I am getting old. In a promising development, however, I recently learned that I can send a text message from my BlackBerry, which does not involve the whole irritating three-letters-per-key situation. The other day I texted my son from my BlackBerry until he stopped replying. So perhaps there is hope for me. If I could just learn how to sort my e-mail by folders, maybe I'd feel fifteen again.

Young and restless: Your children at the dinner table. Based on my experience as the mother of three boys, eating dinner as a family is so stressful (see *Unhappy hour,* p. 216) that it feels like it should be part of the workday. And yet we persist.

Your Non-Retirement Retirement, an Owner's Manual: The self-help book that someone needs to write for working mothers who feel ambivalent about working for the forty years they have been on the job, but who feel even more ambivalent about not working at all.

Yesterday I had lunch with my dear friend Jane, a fellow magazine editor and one of the top women in my life. She is tops for a number of reasons, including the fact that she is older, smarter, and funnier than I am, and she almost always seems to have the right answer, no matter what the question. She is both cynical and sentimental, which I find to be the most winning combination, and she has read all the classics I still haven't gotten to, some more than once. She introduces topics like the Crimean War into casual lunchtime conversation, as she did yesterday, which makes me both idolize and fear her. She has a few friends who are quite famous and others who are quite rich and many who are neither, and she treats all of us exactly the same way: that is, for each of us she is president of the fan club. There is very little you could want from a friend that Jane does not deliver.

Another admirable thing about Jane is that she loves to work, but she doesn't really want to work very *hard*. Pretty much every career decision she's ever made has been with two goals in mind: one, to be able to spend plenty of time with her son, and two, to leave the office before cocktail hour. She will work only with people she likes, and if there is someone in the organization who does not meet with her approval, she will find a way to get that person moved out of her orbit. And so she also appears to have magical powers.

Currently Jane's company is in a bit of turmoil, and she is working about 25 percent harder than she would like. Naturally her thoughts have turned to the idea of not working at all. Jane has cooked up this half-baked scheme to have her husband do a lot of work in Europe so that she can quit her job and move there and pass the time drinking good wine, thinking big thoughts, and reading all of Dickens yet again. I told Jane I thought that sounded like an interesting plan but wondered if they could actually afford it. "Well," she explained, "we talked to our guy at Fidelity and found out that we have enough money to live on until I'm eighty, and then I'm going to kill myself."

Like many of the working mothers I know, Jane is really good at what she does, really loves what she does, and yet talks longingly and with some frequency about quitting. In fact, I would venture to say that most of my working-mom friends fantasize much more about leaving the workforce than they do about being promoted; they just keep getting promoted anyway, despite themselves. And yet we also all talk about how we might die if we ever stopped working (see *Family-friendly living,* p. 73). Does this dichotomy exist for men? I'm not so sure. For many women in our culture, to work or not to work looks like a choice from the get-go, and so there is the constant wondering if your choice has been the right one. The men I know were not raised to believe they had that choice. So perhaps it is only men who retire; women merely leave the workforce to pursue a path they didn't choose in the beginning.

Once you take financial necessity out of the equation, you might say I view my working life as a stage, a fun exercise that I'm going to pursue until it seems too stupid or boring to continue. When I consider all the things I wish I were doing instead of working—and despite the fact that I love my job, the list is endless—I harbor the persistent, naïve belief that I will get to those things later. It's not not working that I want; I just have an insatiable curiosity about so many things that working gets in the way of. Think of the rude awakening that faces me when I get the gold watch at age sixty-five and realize, *Oh no, I'm sixty-five years old! Is it too late to have more children?* Then maybe I will have to move to Europe to live with Jane, if she hasn't killed herself yet.

If I'm not having more children when I'm sixty-five, what will I do? Will I sleep until 8:00? Will I watch the six-hour BBC production of *Pride and Prejudice* once a month, which seems wonderful and indulgent and must happen during the day because my husband has a limited tolerance for movies with characters in waistcoats? Will I raise award-winning roses or make my own sausage or learn to knit, or just sell everything so my husband and I can travel around the world?

Will I be bored? That is the scariest thought. Just as Jane has made many of her career decisions with her son and the cocktail hour in mind, many of my decisions are driven by fear of boredom. It is a powerful motivator. I have spent so much of my adult life going fast; what will it feel like to slow down? I talk constantly about wanting a life that's less complicated, but as soon as I get closer to that, I come up with some harebrained idea to make it crazier again. (The latest? That we should get another dog, which I need like I need a hole in my head.)

After fear of boredom comes fear of regret. If my days are relatively empty and my brain is relatively idle, will I spend too much time looking back and wishing I had done many things differently? Starting with motherhood, the biggest regret magnet of them all. In his book *Losing Mum and Pup,* Christopher Buckley describes being with his mother on her deathbed and telling her, "I forgive you." Oh my God. Am I doing all I can to avoid *that?* I have this small but persistent fear based on an interaction my friend Cindi had with her four-year-old daughter as she was leaving one night for a business trip. Her daughter followed her to the elevator of their building and as Cindi stood in the elevator and her daughter stood in the hall, her daughter said desperately, "I love you, I love you, I don't know what else to say, but I love you!" And then the elevator doors closed, and Cindi was off to the airport. You don't need to be going to Paris to experience this; our entire work lives are a constant leave-taking from our children. Am I going to regret having left them every single day? On my deathbed, is one of my sons going to say to me, "Mom, I forgive you for working?" Perhaps. And I will reply, "I love you, I love you, I don't know what else to say, but I love you."

Zero-sum living

Zip it

Zuzu's petals phenomenon

Zero-sum living:

If you try to get in shape, you will never be well rested.

If you get enough sleep, you will always have a little tummy.

If you have too many enjoyable "date nights" with your husband, you will wish you never had kids.

(If you have dinner every night with three young boys, you may also wish you never had kids.)

If you dress to get promoted like all those career-building self-help books recommend, your colleagues will think you are putting on airs and band together to hate you, and you will never get promoted.

If you are a woman who is too tough, people will say you're a bitch and no one will want to work for you.

If you are a woman who is not tough enough, people will say you are a bad leader and no one will want to work for you.

If you wear flats to work, you will look dumpy but smart.

If you wear high heels to work, you will look pretty but stupid.

If you are too good a team player, people will think you are a
   pushover.
If you hire your CEO's goddaughter as a summer intern, that
   means you are a suck-up.
If you don't hire your CEO's goddaughter as a summer
   intern, you clearly don't know how the world works.

Zip it: What you must tell yourself when you are at that con-
versational tipping point when you really want to say the thing
that will anger your husband (leading to an argument: half
an hour), make your child storm out of the room (consoling a
teenager: half the evening), or cause a coworker to think you
are unreasonable (proving you can be easy to work with: half
your life). True, we all did learn that honesty is the best policy.
It's just not always the smartest policy, and certainly not the
most efficient.

Zuzu's petals phenomenon: The ultimate reality check, or the
sign that nothing matters more than your children. This is a
necessary, sometimes shaming reminder from a higher power
that you need to have your head examined if you actually think
that, say, skipping your child's piano recital for a work meeting
is a wise choice.

Everyone is familiar with the moment in *It's a Wonderful
Life* when George Bailey comes through his life-and-death
ordeal to find, still in his pocket, the petals from the flower
that his daughter Zuzu wanted him to fix. For George, dis-
covering the petals at the end of the movie signals a promise

of redemption; no matter how he has screwed up, his kids will give him another chance. They know which end is up and, now, so does he.

Working motherhood is a process of constant negotiation— between your personal and professional identities, between your need to nurture your kids and please your boss, between you and your partner to see who is able to handle more on any given day. You're negotiating even with yourself: if I stay at the office until after the kids are in bed, I'll go home early on Friday; if I take three hours at lunch to get my hair cut and colored, I'll check my e-mail every ten minutes; and so on. The working mother constantly weighs her job against her home life and makes the best choice in the moment, giving priority to one side or another, depending on the circumstances of the day.

Over the years I have made hundreds of bad choices, and I will make hundreds more before I'm done. It's all too easy to extrapolate when you feel you must put work before family; you can rationalize any decision to the point that the family actually benefits when work wins out. (If I miss this client dinner it will look bad to my boss, which means I will never get promoted, which means we will not be able to save enough for college, and so we should cut back on expenses now and cancel the kids' piano lessons. Which is unthinkable! Therefore I'd better attend the client dinner for the sake of my children.) There are times you'd certainly *rather* be at work; for all the mothers out there who get a headache just contemplating a planetarium trip with a class of twenty third graders—well, I feel your pain. But on most days, you would prefer to be with your children.

You need work to provide for them, and the contrast of work to home life just makes children feel all the more miraculous.

It is easy to forget such miracles in the busyness and tedium of daily life. It is easy to forget that you would do anything for your children. Particularly as your children grow older, and their need for you grows quieter and less immediate, it is easy to forget that work can be like a siren's song in its allure. And, like a siren's song, obsession with work can lead you down the path of destruction. This is where Zuzu's petals come in. George Bailey had to nearly commit suicide and be rescued by an angel in order to put things in perspective. Presumably the rest of us would rather skip that step.

In my purse I carry a little headless Lego man, one escapee of the eighty or so that seem to reproduce nightly in my sons' bedroom. He lives in the small side compartment with my cell phone and work ID and Blistex — that is, the priority zone of my purse. The Lego man started out in the pocket of a raincoat that I wore one day seven years ago to the final interview for my current job. As I walked up the street to the meeting, I kept my hand in my pocket and held on tight to that little Lego guy. He was my Zuzu's petals, the silent reminder that this was only a job, after all, and that no matter what happened, there would still be seventy-nine of his friends waiting for me at home, along with a child who wanted nothing more than for me to sit down on the floor with him and marvel at the world he had constructed.

I ended up getting the job, and both out of gratitude to the Lego guy and a small dose of superstition, I moved him from the raincoat to my purse, where he continues to watch over me. Most of the time I forget he's there, until I can't find my Blistex and I find him instead. And then I pause, if only for a minute, to think about the three boys who brought Legos into my life, and enriched it more than I ever could have imagined. My experience as a working mother remains one of trial and error. Still, I've had mostly good luck since the day the Lego man appeared in my pocket, and so I remain determined to do everything I can to protect my little plastic friend.

Acknowledgments

For their advice, guidance, inspiration, and support, I would like to thank: Lani Adler, Karen Andrews, Kristin Appenbrink, Sylvia Auton, Jim Baker, Tracy Behar, Jane Berentson, Debbie Bologno, Silvia Carroll, Janet Chan, Kris Connell, Mary Crotty, Olivia Dunn, Sarah Kate Ellis, Heather Fain, Janet Froelich, Carrie Goldin, Janice Goldklang, Noelle Howey, John Huey, Mimi Humphrey, Sarah Humphreys, Chloe Jones, Sharene Jones, Bucky Keady, Chrissie Lawrence, Elizabeth Leckie, Cindi Leive, Dan Meador, Jackie Monk, Martha Nelson, Richard Pine, Amanda Potters, Katy Reitz, Deb Richman, Heather Rizzo, Kim Robertson, Dean Robinson, Glen Robinson, Jenny Robinson, Kay Robinson, Christina Rodriguez (both of you), Steve Sachs, Raylene Salthouse, Ann Savarino, Tamara Stewart, Claire van Ogtrop, Connie van Ogtrop, Piet van Ogtrop, Valerie van Ogtrop, Kevin White, Ellene Wundrok, and Jayne Yaffe Kemp.

About the Author

Kristin van Ogtrop is the editor of *Real Simple* magazine. She has held various editorial jobs at other magazines, including *Glamour* and *Vogue*. Her essay "Attila the Honey I'm Home" appeared in the *New York Times* bestseller *The Bitch in the House,* and her blog, "Adventures in Chaos," appears on RealSimple.com. She has a B.A. in English from the University of Virginia and an M.A. in English from Columbia University. When she's not at work, she lives in the suburbs of New York with her (fairly patient) husband, several pets, and three children, whom she loves very much even though they clean their rooms only about once a year.